Real Estate Mistakes

Our Mistakes, Your Success

Second Edition: Newly Revised and Updated

Monika & Vaughan Jazyk

Real Estate Mistakes

Our Mistakes, Your Success

Second Edition: Newly Revised and Updated

Monika & Vaughan Jazyk

The Awakened Press

The Awakened Press
www.theawakenedpress.com

For information about special discounts for bulk purchases, please contact The Awakened Press at books@theawakenedpress.com.
The Awakened Press can bring authors to your live event. For more information or to book an event contact books@theawakenedpress.com or visit our website at www.theawakenedpress.com.

Cover and book design by Kurt A. Dierking II

Printed in Canada and the United States of America
Second edition

ISBN: 979-8-9870434-6-2

Monika and Vaughan Jazyk are a wonderful couple that desire a family first lifestyle that is both attractive and inspiring. They do this by building a business in real estate that can fund itself and is able to give them the time to enjoy the things that matter most. What I appreciate about this fun-filled couple is that they always continue to learn, even though they are in a position to teach. This humility is contagious.

—Rav Toor
Speaker, Investor, and TV Host

Don't let Monika and Vaughan's calm and quiet natures fool you. They are a powerful force who have created a thriving real estate business, driven by their desire to create a great life for their family and help others do the same.

—Julie Broad
Speaker and Bestselling Author, Rev N You Training Inc.

Monika and Vaughan have an undeniable energy that is evident the moment anyone meets them. It takes many years of hard work to get to that level of knowledge of investment properties, finding great deals, and creating strategic partnerships. Look closely at what they do well—and explore the possibilities with them and their team.

—Todor Yordanov
Real Estate Broker Extraordinaire and Bestselling Author
Founder of the Real Estate Network Toronto

The day I met Monika and Vaughan is one I'll never forget. They'll tell you I changed their lives...but the reality is, they changed mine. Up until that point, I had NEVER worked with two people who were so dedicated and driven before, and at the same time so open-minded. You will find they are the most vulnerable, decent, and caring people you will probably ever meet...especially in the real estate world.

There are a lot of "fake it 'till you make its" and people pretending to "live the life" while the truth is, it's crashing down around and inside them. I don't have to tell you that Monika and Vaughan WERE among those people.

That's why you need to read this book. Because you will ride alongside their life. They'll reveal everything (vulnerability) so you and I can benefit from their mistakes (decent and caring). You'll see how they never give up, face fear head on, and plough through adversity like no other people I've met.

That night I met them, Monika and Vaughan, who were then complete strangers, were THE MOST vulnerable people in the room...including my coaching clients. And THAT'S why they're successful. They are willing to learn from others' mistakes, and they are willing to step up and admit their own faults.
And now, you have their personal journal in front of you. Don't waste this information. As you read through these stories, think carefully about how you would have reacted. Would you come out the other end with your head held just as high? The answer for me is "NO" a lot of the time.

And that's why they continue to inspire me. That's how they constantly change my life. And if you let them, they'll change yours, too.

Great Speed Forward.
—Joey Ragona
Bestselling Author, Speaker, Real Estate Business Freedom Training and Coaching

To our business coach and friend, Joey Ragona.
Without your guidance, support, and never-ending challenges,
this book would have never been written.

Contents

Foreword

By Mike Wolf

As a real estate investor for the past twenty-six years, I've seen a lot of people come and go from the industry. This industry, unfortunately, is filled with a lot of greed and I see a lot of "gurus" taking advantage of people's hard-earned money in exchange for worthless, or dated, information.

When I heard that Monika and Vaughan Jazyk were writing a book, I became very excited because it's time to change the reputation of the industry. These two are the right people to do that.

I've had the pleasure of knowing this couple for quite some time, and I can tell you that they are the real deal. They are a power team with a wealth of information, always looking out for the best interests of their clients and doing things for the right reason.

I always look forward to my visits to Toronto as I enjoy hearing what Monika and Vaughan are up to and watching them serve the people who rely on them. I've also witnessed the two grow with their real estate investing and how they continue to share their ever-expanding knowledge.

I strongly recommend reading this book from cover to cover—and then, most importantly, *take action.*

Learn from their triumphs, and more importantly, the places where they made mistakes. *The best way to learn how to practice the science of real estate is from others' missteps—not by making your own.* I believe this book will serve you well.

Do not let this become "shelf-help."

To Your Success!
—**Mike Wolf**
International Speaker, Author, and Mentor
MikeWolfMastery.com

Preface

I would like to start off this book with a warning.

This is NOT a "how-to" book.

Reading this book will NOT teach you all the secrets in real estate.

I am not a guru, a billionaire, a member of NASA or Mensa...heck, I don't even know what my IQ is. The intention is NOT to relay my high levels of wisdom and expertise. I am an everyday gal who was sick of getting everyday results with mutual funds and bank products, so I decided to invest in real estate.

There are way too many books and seminars that focus on the highs, the successes, and the glories of business and real estate. This book is giving you the *very real mistakes* made by novice investors after they decide to take the plunge and start investing.

This is the real, raw journey of our investments in REAL estate.

As you're reading through the pages of this story and learning about all our mistakes and lessons, you'll realize how much this book will help you avoid both the common AND uncommon mistakes in real estate investing. This book was created to provide you with the opportunity to save money—and help you discover what's important for YOU.

If I knew then what I know now, my real estate journey would have been very different than it is today. I would certainly not be able to share these insights and challenges to help reveal the decisions that will be right for you.

If you are a newbie investor on the fence or ready to make a purchase, this book is a MUST read as it will help you avoid making some very common REAL ESTATE MISTAKES!

You may have already started investing and even made some mistakes yourself! If this is the case, may this book be a source of consolation that you are NOT alone, and an inspiration that you can get through this.

My hope is that you achieve all your personal and financial goals, and have the courage to move forward on your real estate investing journey without having to experience the tumultuous trials and tribulations we went through.

If our story can help you avoid even *one* of these mistakes, I would consider this book a success!

Now, on to the adventures...

Chapter 1

The One That Got Away

Let me take you back twenty years ago. We were young, straight out of school, in the beginning of our new romance. We were open to new opportunities, life was good, and we were receptive to all it had to offer.

Until we were hit, head on, with an emotion all too common in adulthood...

FEAR.

The sad truth is, if we hadn't been so fearful...if we had stayed hopeful, open, and receptive, we probably would have been millionaires at twenty-four years old.

This is only the beginning of our cautionary tale into the mistakes we made in real estate investing. With open eyes, excitement, and a newbie's lust for making money, we were hungry for opportunity and instant success. We really had no idea what it takes to be successful in this industry—or even what "success" really meant to us.

Let me take you back to Jandakot, Western Australia. On a bright, crisp day I remember opening the newspaper and seeing an ad for blocks of land for sale in a suburb just outside of Perth, Western Australia. At the time we were living there we really had no clue about *land*, land developments, or even real estate, for that matter. But what we *did* know was what a "blue-chip" golf course estate development was—and had grand plans about living there.

My now-husband and I responded to the ad almost immediately. Soon we found ourselves at the building site—which didn't look like much at the time, aside from makeshift roads winding through mounds of dirt, dotted with pegs from surveyors outlining the soon-to-be dream homes of potential buyers like us.

Everything was moving in slow motion...it was like a dream. It was *happening*, but not really happening. Almost like we were playing grown-ups in a make-believe play.

What I DO remember is handing over the deposit money to the salesman (who was also the developer), to reserve our block of land...*FIVE HUNDRED DOLLARS!*

When I write this sum today I laugh, but I still remember the sinking feeling of handing over that money. It was A LOT of money for us at the time. What coursed through me was an intense, lingering, gut-twisting fear of never getting that $500 back.

The exchange of this sum of money is what I remember most. To us, it wasn't just the monetary value, it was what the $500 represented. It was the fear of the unknown. Fear of being ripped off. Fear of looking stupid. Lack of faith that this piece of dirt and all of its neighbors would actually be transformed into this "blue-chip" golf course estate community.

Fueled with youthful optimism, we skimmed through these short-lived negative feelings and persevered.

The land was sold separately, making this neighborhood even more distinct as opposed to the cookie-cutter homes prevalent in the surrounding suburban neighborhoods. All the houses in the development were to be custom built. What we really wanted was a four-bedroom, four-bathroom. In Australia, this is rather luxurious because having even two bathrooms can be considered a luxury due to consistent water shortages. It was awe-inspiring and we were *doing it*.

We made the decision to buy that very same day. So, our next stop was to find a builder.

One sunny Saturday we browsed for model homes and met an American sales representative. I always referred to him as "Ringo Starr" because of his liveliness and cheerful attitude. "Ringo Starr" was amazing and not only helped us find a model home we liked, but helped us completely redesign the model until we ended up with a 3500-square-foot bungalow with a walkout basement, exercise room, media room, *and* all sorts of extras to build a house fit for a superstar like the actual *Ringo Starr*...all for the whopping price of $120,000! *We were on fire!*

Our next stop was to obtain financing for this grown-up dream that was fast becoming a reality.

I remember us going to the bank in Perth city and speaking to the lady about loans and mortgages. Our knowledge about mortgages was nonexistent. I remember sitting calmly, looking at my surroundings and thinking about what a gorgeous bank this was before shaking her hand and thanking her for the approval of a $200,000 mortgage...along with a personal line of credit for the $20,000 to cover the amount we were short, just as if this was a natural thing.

We thought this was the "normal" way loans were administered—that everyone gets approved! We were on our way to building our dream home...isn't this the way life should be?

Cue the naysayers—AKA, Mom and Dad.

Prior to building our new home, we decided to return to Canada for a visit over Christmas to share our hopes and dreams with our loved ones. Rather than receiving well wishes, we were peppered with pessimism and negative possible outcomes of "*WHAT IFs*," as well as multiple dire predictions. Although my gut feeling told me their intentions were for our greatest and highest good, the manner in which it was delivered wasn't all that encouraging.

The sinking feeling in the pit of my stomach rushed right back to me—the feeling of looking stupid, making a mistake...losing it all. The feeling of FEAR. And although I do NOT remember what exactly was said, I DO remember getting on a plane, zipping back to Australia, and going straight to the developer to cancel our entire transaction.

Immediately we returned to collect what I feared losing most: our precious $500 and the risk of being swindled.

To this day I can picture the look in the developer's eyes when he asked us if we were sure. And from what I could see it wasn't because *he* was losing out on a sale—it was because he knew that *we* were missing out on a golden opportunity; a game changer that would likely set us up for life.

It all crumbled away because of FEAR.

...A couple years later, life was still good. We had to put the past behind us.

Still young, newly married; more educated as I was completing my Master of Arts in Teaching; living in a beachfront rental home in Broome, Western Australia, with a healthy baby boy bouncing on my knee.

As a casual afterthought, I decided to Google the name of the estate development in Jandakot. After I entered the search and scanned the results, what I saw on the screen was not only pictures of what the blue-chip golf course estate area looked like—*but price tags on these homes ranging from $1.5 to $2 MILLION DOLLARS.*

My heart got lodged in my throat.

The sensation I experienced almost knocked me off my stool and could be described as being hit by a Mack Truck.

...THIS feeling was worse than the feeling of fear.

This was the feeling of a *missed opportunity*, and it SUCKED!

Missed opportunity can be described as fear's ugly sister. The devastating thing about missed opportunity is that it's like being slapped in the face. You don't realize how good you have it until it's gone. You tend to feel very unconfident that a similar opportunity will ever come up again. Not only do you get the same sinking feeling in your stomach as you do with the fear, but you're also gulping a heavy dosage of the reality of what you missed out on, and what could have been.

This led to a panicked state of *"making things right."*

In a dazed state I found myself on the phone desperately trying to contact the developer, who was nowhere to be found.

Even if we did find him, it wouldn't have been the same. The prices wouldn't have been as low as they were before, the location would not have been as good, and the list goes on and on.

It appears the stars were aligned for the duration of this adventure as everything came together so seamlessly before we interfered. The puzzle was broken and pieces were missing. And we all know the importance of putting the right pieces together in a puzzle—you can't force them to fit. As is the game of life.

Opportunity lost. Lesson learned. We could have been millionaires in our mid-twenties on one real estate transaction. But the opportunity got away because of fear.

To this day we've never lived in a house like the one we designed in such a seamless location for such a great price...and possibly never will.

The hard lesson we learned from this experience changed our attitudes toward real estate and toward fear, allowing us to move ahead in our real estate investment journey.

There are two major points to this story; both are common elements that you WILL face on your real estate journey. And if they are *not* addressed, they WILL likely stop you.

The first is that *fear of the unknown* has more consequences than we realize because we rarely see the opportunity we missed. In our case, I SAW it. And you probably "see" missed opportunities for buying real estate at X dollars a few years ago—because right now the market may be higher. The truth is, you'll be saying that a few years from now if you don't take a chance on your dreams and invest today.

The second point is that the further you move away from the status quo—meaning that you're doing something that your friends and family probably have zero faith in, or would ever risk themselves—the more you'll get "free advice" on why it's a "bad idea."

Unless your family and friends are involved with a successful organization, go with YOUR gut, not someone else's fear of crushing your future.

Chapter 2

The Road to Hell is Paved with Good Intentions

Anyone who has gone to any real estate training course, be it a three-day session or even a free information night, has learned the importance of having a "WHY." I distinctly recall the salesperson at a free session I attended a while back, describing how investing in real estate for fast cars or to have a Learjet wasn't an option; but instead, for family, to be able to pay for your child's wedding abroad, and to fly the entire family over to enjoy the celebrations.

I'll also never forget how the trainer of our three-day weekend course spread photos of his family all over the podium as a reminder of *why* he was there.

Gone are the days of Tom Vu in front of his mansion surrounded by young women. Marketers seem to have figured out what *really* works by aiming toward more achievable goals that people can relate to. One main goal being family.

This strategy really works! It especially worked for us. The pitch tugged on my heartstrings and helped me create our own *why*.

Let's veer back to Australia for a moment before the baby boy was bouncing on my knee. Just before his birth I was still licking my wounds from our real estate tragedy, but getting ready to return to the classroom to complete a twelve-week teaching practicum for my Master of Teaching. I began this two-year program when I was newly engaged, and was a diligent student receiving top grades, even working as a tutor and lecturer part-time. Over the course of this two-year period we were married, and soon I was expecting our first son. As I was continuing with my studies I returned to the classroom just one week after giving birth to him to complete my final exams.

When practically everybody else in my program went straight to the classroom to complete their twelve-week teaching practicum (which would qualify them to be full-time teachers), I went back to my house to be a full-time mom.

I had twelve months to complete this practicum, but seeing that our baby was only three weeks old then, it didn't seem like a good time. I had eight months to learn all about parenting and being home with a new baby. Being so young and inexperienced, not expecting the hardships of this twenty-four-hour job being a mom (all the celebrities make it look like a breeze!) the surrounding walls closed in around me fast and I was looking forward to being back in the classroom *achieving*...moving forward...receiving actual grades for my performance, unlike being at home.

Aside from your child being alive at the end of the day, there is no type of evaluation for being a mom! So when he was eight months old, off I went—twelve weeks in the classroom teaching fifty-two Grade 7 students so I could complete my degree and become a full-time teacher.

Two weeks into it I realized I was DEAD WRONG. I was affected by separation anxiety from my child. It is not natural for mothers to be away from their baby. People don't really talk about the internal longing...the physical pain in the pit of your stomach and the all-encompassing preoccupation that changes you and prevents you from being the same person you were before children. I couldn't focus, and soon I was no longer the high achieving, A-plus, supersonic student I used to be.

I'd leave the best part of me at daycare at 7:00 a.m. every morning.

Then I'd rush out early at 3:00 p.m. every afternoon, when I should have been doing all the "extras" during my working life (classroom prep, staff meetings, extra credit reports)—resulting in so-so grades AND so-so parenting due to the mental and physical exhaustion of *trying to do it all.*

Soon this phantom pain metamorphosed from an emotional state into a full-blown ulcer, causing even further distress. Twenty-seven years old and I was falling apart mentally and physically. I wondered, is this what it was like to be a full-time working mom?

After experiencing this phenomenon firsthand, I knew this was NOT the life for me. I shared this confession with my husband late one night in the hospital, during this difficult time when our son was receiving treatment from a bacterial infection he had caught in daycare. He shared my sentiments exactly.

Family first. Work second.

And that is the way we moved forward in the following years.

I did complete my Master of Teaching. I worked as a teacher (part-time). And I did stay home 80% of the time with our little son...and then three more beautiful children we added to our brood over the years.

Although we were achieving our PERSONAL goals, we were living in a FINANCIAL nightmare.

After the completion of my master's degree, we left Australia to live in Canada to be closer with family and to become homeowners. The cost of living was high, and only having one steady income was a struggle. With most of my time devoted to being a stay-at-home mom, one of my jobs was managing the family finances, and it was easy to see that more was going out than was coming in.

Our main concern was paying for future expenses. Primarily, funding our retirement and university tuition for *four kids*! How were we going to fund these expenses on *one salary*, with the cost of inflation and day-to-day living, *without* compromising my choice of being a stay-at-home mom? Although my kids were getting older, it appeared they needed me even more!

I started creating budgets and read up on financial strategies to create income—real estate being one of them.

We followed what I call today "the government hamster wheel," reducing our expenses drastically so we could save 10% in RRSPs, RESPs, and TFSAs.

Imagine my dismay after realizing we were getting minimal, if not *negative* returns. We needed to do something different—something that generated immediate income while creating wealth for future costs. I knew there had to be a better way and fortunately, out of all the financial strategies I was studying, real estate seemed to always be a frontrunner.

Although real estate appeared to be the answer, we did not know where to start and felt like we didn't have the money. Until, finally, "*someday*" became "*one day.*"

Our financial planner introduced us to a consolidated mortgage which allowed us access to the equity in our home. We used these funds to get started on our investment journey. Looking back on the Australian incident, I felt a pang of fear as the memories trickled back in the corner of my mind's eye. With newfound excitement and motivation, I shook it off. This journey was FAR from over.

Although it may seem tripe, the importance of a WHY is paramount in real estate investing. It will keep you focused and true to your core. It will help get you through common obstacles such as *analysis paralysis,* times of doubt, and the well-intentioned warnings from family, friends, and the media.

But having a *general* WHY is not enough. Your WHY, like all goals that can become a reality, needs to be CRYSTAL CLEAR and LASER-LIKE, otherwise distraction and disillusionment can easily kick in and cause you to lose focus.

In our case, the challenge was that our WHY was blurry. We knew we wanted to invest in real estate to create wealth for our family, but our goals were not specific.

Looking back, I would go through our business coach Joey Ragona's activity featured in the Appendix to establish SPECIFIC GOALS. Be sure to use this fundamental resource for yourself (see Appendix). As our journey continued, we used this strategy I'm sharing with you to figure out *our* exact WHY:

To buy each child an investment property to fund their university education.

Once this goal was established, the trees cleared and a golden path led the way in all of our real estate investment decisions.

German philosopher Friedrich Nietzsche once said, "*He who has a why can endure any how.*"

Knowing your *why* is an important first step in figuring out *how* to achieve the goals that excite you and create a life you enjoy living (versus merely surviving!). Indeed, only when you know your "*why*" will you find the courage to take the risks needed to get ahead, stay motivated when the chips are down, and move your life into an entirely new, more challenging, and more rewarding trajectory.

When you really sit down and figure out the power of your *purpose* to tap reserves of energy, determination, and courage, you will have a mission that's clear. Your goal will be compelling. Your focus will be laser-like.

Without clarity we can so easily fall into disillusionment, distraction, and a quiet sense of despair.

Chapter 3

Building a House Without a Solid Foundation

APPROVED!

MORTGAGE OBTAINED!

Time to start house shopping!

After our magical money appeared from the bank via our consolidated mortgage, we received a huge dose of courage and were ready to move forward. Little did we know that investing in real estate is A LOT more than simply buying and selling properties.

We still had no idea how things really worked in terms of a mortgage approval, area selection, types of properties, property management, and ROI (Return on Investment)—or even what ROI really was. We didn't even know all the reasons why real estate is a good investment. All we knew about real estate investing is that your income needs to exceed your expenses...and if you own any additional property aside from your primary residence, you will appear to be a big shot!

Our first step was to find a mortgage broker to see how much we would qualify for a loan. We didn't select this mortgage broker based on references, research, or even after a phone interview. At the time, we had no idea about the complexity of mortgages and how all mortgage brokers are *not* created equal. We simply knew this person as someone who lived in our neighborhood and decided to utilize their services.

There we were...at our dining room table with a local mortgage broker discussing our options. *Property A:* a ski vacation rental condominium in a popular Canadian vacation spot, Blue Mountain, for $120K. *Property B:* a single-family home in Timmins, Ontario, Canada, for $40K.

The mortgage broker literally snort-laughed when we mentioned the Timmins property, saying that obtaining a mortgage in a place like that—under one thousand square feet and in *that* price point—was "IMPOSSIBLE"; and how Property A was a much better option, as "everyone knows and loves Blue Mountain and skiing is so much fun" (or something of the sort). So we proceeded with the intention to buy a ski vacation rental for a relatively low price (in comparison to the price of our primary residence), which we could make income from renting out to vacationers and also use for ourselves and our own vacations throughout the year. What a perfect first investment!

We hunted down a real estate agent in the Blue Mountain area with a quick Google search and met her at the property we were interested in. Together, with our baby in tow, we viewed different units in the complex and decided on a mountainside unit that we could add value to with a little bit of paint and cosmetic upgrades. With the help of our real estate agent, we put in an offer and it was accepted!

We were on our way!

After A LOT of paperwork and a home inspection, we removed the conditions written in the offer (meaning that by law we had to close on this property by the agreed-upon closing date) and proceeded to financing, as we were approved for a mortgage, right? *Wrong!*

Shortly after all conditions were removed, our mortgage agent alerted us that we needed to come up with *more* money down! It appeared that we were *not* approved, after all!

It ended up being a panicked situation. We had very little understanding about what was fully happening. We desperately scrambled to find funds with a potential lawsuit from the sellers looming over us if we did not close on this property!

I couldn't understand why this was happening. How can someone analyze your information, say you're approved, advise you to remove conditions, and then all of a sudden say you are not approved?

After a very teary and confused phone call, I was in hysterics. According to the mortgage broker, our mortgage agent turned out to be inexperienced and made a crucial mistake somewhere in the application. To this day I'm not really sure what happened. At the end of the day, the broker pulled some serious strings and helped us save the deal.

It was a close call for our family. We could have been burned alive easily, without really being fully aware of the situation. But after all was said and done, we now owned our very first investment property.

Everything started off smoothly. We transformed our tired-looking 1970s ski condo to a chic and luxurious vacation rental. I worked with a local contractor and designer who helped us renovate on a budget. We soon found a local property management company specializing in vacation rentals through a reference from our real estate agent to help us rent the place out when we weren't using it.

We were ready to start enjoying our luxury ski rental and make money when we were not using it! Right?

So wrong.

The major problem was, aside from staying there one night, we NEVER used it! The place looked so great that we didn't want to ruin it!

Plus, once we decided the house would be a rental property, we became aware that if we were using it, we were losing out on potential rent, which eliminated any chance of enjoyment. This was the first lesson we learned:

Business and personal do NOT mix.

I became obsessed with filling the unit whenever it was vacant, taking it upon myself to advertise on Kijiji and other social media networks. Instead of letting the income roll in, I felt the stress of filling vacancies, spending hours a day posting and managing ads and haggling with vacationers who were determined to rent the condo for the lowest price possible. This impeded on my personal time, making it almost a full-time job.

During the prime seasons (December-March and July-September), this unit did very well despite the fact that it was competing with hundreds of other similar units in the area. I had no idea about vacancy rates and how they really worked. But during the shoulder season (April-June and October-November) rentals were few and far between. Unfortunately, our expenses still needed to be paid every month, despite the lack of income and hours of time put in trying to cover vacancies.

It is vital to remember that mortgage payments, condo fees, property taxes and utilities—including water, hydro, gas and cable—require payments *all year long. This is regardless if your unit is rented or if you are using it.*

We also quickly realized that *our condo fees exceeded our mortgage payments!* True, condo fees pay for a lot of property maintenance expenses. However, you still have to make this payment every month, *whether or not you've paid off your property in full.* We were well aware what this number was thanks to our real estate agent connecting us with a lawyer specializing in condominiums, but didn't think too much of it until we actually saw it on paper. Not much fun.

After a full year of dealing with the high-maintenance cost of the condo fees, a temperamental property with high expenses and a fluctuating income, we put it back on the market...where it sat for two more years.

Looks like a lot of people saw something else coming that we didn't. Due to our excitement to buy and emotionally connecting to something we personally loved, we failed to do our *Real Estate 101* homework, mainly because we had little to no real estate education at the time.

The property FINALLY sold *for the exact same price we bought it for.*

After reviewing the numbers, in a financial perspective we broke even after two more years of having it sit, but the lessons we learned far outweighed the financial implications.

It was a frustrating experience because even though it was renting out while we were trying to sell it, it was a time-sucker and something we desperately wanted to get rid of. I had no intention of continuing to work around the clock operating it as a ski rental.

Although we were still lacking formal real estate education at this point, our hands-on experience from the Blue Mountain episode made us realize: a) the importance of using a local mortgage broker familiar with the type of housing in the area, rather than using one mortgage broker for everything (unless they have connections and familiarity with that particular area); and b) the importance of selecting a real estate agent in the area who can be your eyes and ears when you are investing out of town. (Did I mention Timmins is nine hours away from downtown Toronto, Canada's major metropolis?)

Two months after the Blue Mountain purchase, we had bought another property. Excited and motivated to continue our dream in real estate investing, we put in an offer for a small single-family home for $40K in Timmins, Ontario, Canada. The financing went remarkably smooth since we used a different mortgage broker operating out of the same area. We chose this city because of the low purchase prices in the region, as well as the higher-than-average rental rates. My husband Vaughan and I also had firsthand experience with these types of mining towns, as my hubby grew up in a similar type of town in Western Australia where the shortage of housing combined with the remoteness led to a demand for housing, driving up the prices and rental rates.

When it came to putting in an offer for the Timmins house, we selected a real estate agent in the area. It was a bank sale house that was listed for $29K. The owner had stopped making mortgage payments on the home, so the bank took the property back and was selling it for a price below fair market value in exchange for a quick profit.

The appraised value of the house five years prior was $55K. As a result, there were A LOT of parties interested in this property. This forced us to participate in our first bidding war to buying our first house in Timmins—SIGHT UNSEEN! We had never actually been to Timmins before to search for homes.

Aside from telephone conversations with our real estate agent, we had never actually met her face-to-face. This can be common when you're exploring the notion of investing in properties that are a distance away from your primary residence. Most interactions with professionals in the area occur over telephone or video conference. We'd also read several books before buying that encouraged buying sight unseen—so the fact that we had never actually MET our agent face-to-face or even viewed the property before we purchased it did not seem too crazy at the time. It actually made us feel like seasoned investors who didn't need to waste our time meeting agents and walking through properties. Plus, she was very knowledgeable and helpful. So we moved forward with submitting an offer.

Our offer was $40K...and we won! The house was ours! We were victorious! And then the real work began.

The house needed extensive renovations, which we also had to manage from a distance. We weren't planning to move to Timmins, especially since we had a young family to take into consideration. The fact that we had small children to care for and an active life in the Toronto area limited our ability to visit our property on a regular basis and made it even more necessary to form a "Timmins Team" to manage all aspects of our investment.

Creating a Timmins Team proved to be an enormous task considering we basically had to gut the entire property and create a brand-new house. Renovations included a new kitchen, new bath, and a fresh basement with the addition of a second bedroom. Not to mention it needed an updated roof, rewired electrical, and the removal of a tree that had grown into the side of the house.

Remember that during all of this, we still hadn't even seen the house.

From a distance, still never seeing this home in person, we renovated an entire house. As easy as this sounds, the experience was anything BUT easy.

We hired contractors that walked off the job mid-project, and electricians who came to the house saying they completed the work when they never actually did. Our saving grace was our real estate agent who acted as our eyes and ears in Timmins. She was the closest thing I had to a reliable source and I depended on her recommendations to the workers, her opinion on how things were going, and if work was actually getting done.

After many mistakes and setbacks, we ended up finding a contractor who renovated the entire house and acted as a project manager to oversee the trades coming in and out. He also completed the job right on budget...$10K. In my opinion, this was a huge success as we bought a house way under fair market value. Our extensive renovations added further value to the home (forced equity) for a low cost, tripling the overall value of the home.

We had no idea who was going to manage this property and put tenants in it once the project was complete. Our next step was to find a property manager to find good, reliable tenants who would pay fair market rent (in this area at the time, it was about $900 per month). We started searching for a property manager before the renovations started and "met" some real characters over the phone. After interviewing them, the idea was that our real estate agent would tell us her professional opinion of them when she saw them in person.

The first person seemed great! The individual was originally from the Greater Toronto Area (something in common!), was well spoken, and was currently managing over fifty homes in Timmins. But when I asked for references, there were none to be found. And when it came time to view our house it was a big, hot mess. According to our agent, this person had a bad reputation in the property management field. So the interview process continued alongside the renovations. Miraculously, would you believe our contractor volunteered for this position? He and his wife also owned a property management company. *Finally*—a trusted source we could count on!

While all of this was happening (acting as a vacation rental travel agent and managing house flips from afar), we managed to find the time and energy to purchase yet *another* house in Timmins. This would be our third investment property. We still had funds in our line of credit and had buying power to purchase more homes. At the time we felt like we were on a roll and on our way to becoming seasoned real estate investors. *This is what investors do,* we thought. *They buy multiple properties one after the other! All in a time span of three short months! Financial freedom, here we come!*

The main attraction to this second property in Timmins was the price point of $40K! We were also becoming familiar with this type of housing. Little did we know we were inadvertently creating a real estate model by buying the same type of property for the same price point, with relatively the same returns, which is the main premise of our real estate business today. It was a tired house, but we decided to put an offer in and leave it in "as is" condition for it was livable. Once again, we put our complete faith in the real estate agent and bought sight unseen.

The pictures revealed a great house on a prime lot—but images don't reveal everything. Nor do home inspection reports. One of the only accuracies of the home inspection report was that it mentioned the lack of basement. The report failed to mention the rotting cribbing (the wooden setting the property is built on) and the fact that the house was literally sinking into the ground, rendering it basically lopsided. It also did not reveal how small the bedrooms actually were (you could hardly fit a bed in them) or the cost of baseboard heating in a city that reaches forty degrees below freezing for the majority of winter.

Although tenants pay for utilities, high bills that compete with their monthly rent often lead to a high turnover. And guess who ends up covering these bills when tenants leave? If you guessed the owner (AKA us) you're bang on.

We were excited to have a third home, but a bit put off with the real estate agent who didn't take these issues into account at the time of our purchase, merely stating, "What did you expect for $40K?" We felt our long-distance relationship with her was coming to an end, but understandably as agents don't really like to work with clients who are buying cheaper homes—because they typically work just as hard, if not even harder, to close these deals and their commissions can be pennies. The same went with our relationship with our property manager. He claimed he was finding potential tenants, yet he failed to give us any details on their background checks, nor did he provide any kind of formal agreement. When he asked me for power of attorney, which would give him full control over both properties, my gut said: *RUN!*

And my gut was right. Because when we found our new real estate agent who referred us to a professional property management team (that we met and interviewed in person), we discovered that the former property manager was a total quack, who didn't screen tenants properly just to get them in quickly...and believe me, it was a *fight* to get our money!

Three completely different types of properties in three months. One facelift, one rehab, and one turnkey that needed a rehab but we couldn't fund it. The lessons we learned were priceless.

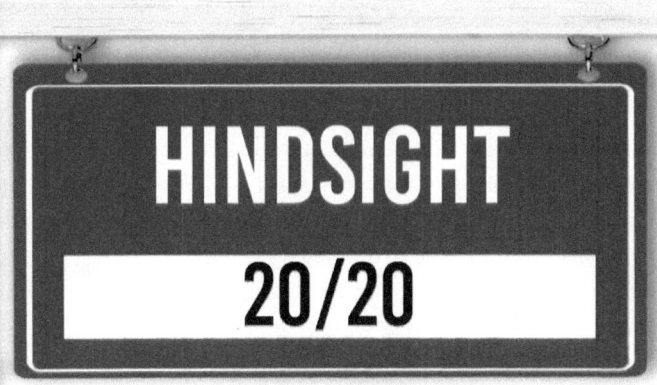

Our first lesson is one I still wrestle with today:

There is NO personal in business.

If at any time during your real estate journey you're putting YOURSELF in the property, it is NOT an investment property. Instead, it's a property that you will be using for personal enjoyment and pleasure.

There's nothing wrong with purchasing something for your personal pleasure; but when you intend for the house to make you money, *this is a business transaction.* Combining your personal enjoyments with your real estate business is mixing emotions with facts, and you may run into similar challenges along the way because of your attachment.

An *asset* is something that makes you money. A liability is something that *costs* you money. One of the classic ways we can trick ourselves in this situation is to convince our minds that the potential property is an ASSET, when in reality it is a LIABILITY. This happens more often when you mix personal pleasure with a business transaction. Ensure you're aware of the differences between the two so you can: a) make sure you can afford it; and b) plan accordingly.

If you want to purchase a vacation property, for example, make sure you finance it properly. There are great programs where you can buy second homes in your personal name. We recommend *not* to incorporate with homes that have any personal use involved, but make sure to consult a mortgage professional to review your options.

Do not count on rental income to cover your property. Make sure you can afford it on your *personal budget.* And compare it to the cost of a seasonal rental. Perhaps it would be better to rent a place for three months as opposed to owning it for twelve?

The second lesson is: condos have several additional items that need to be considered, especially in older buildings like we bought, as condo fees are *always there*! Even if your mortgage is paid off, you still have to pay the condo fees. These only go up as the building gets older. Pair this with property assessments that will occur approximately every five years that can be tens of thousands of dollars. You may have to say goodbye to any profits.

The vacation rental market is very temperamental and *NOT recession-proof*. Some people specialize in this market, and that's great. AirBnB and VRBO are huge, and when you look at the price of a rental you may be enticed to do the same. If you're willing to make this your area of specialty and focus only on renting out your vacation rental, you may do very well.

However, even vacation rental specialists would agree with the following:

1) *Be prepared for the shoulder seasons.* Prime seasons may be cash cows, but there will be certain months out of the year that your property will generate little (if any) income. Therefore, it is very important to account for this in your budget and set aside these funds for property expenses during the slow times.

2) *Vacation properties are NOT recession-proof.* When the economy faces a downturn, the first thing people do is cut their leisure and recreational activities. People stop traveling, dining out, and taking vacations, which, in turn, has a negative impact on the vacation rental market.

3) With vacation rentals you may also be faced with high vacancy rates in the area and competing with several other vacation rentals of which the landlords are likely discounting their prices. And if you think your vacation rental can sell easily, be mindful of my fourth point:

4) *Most vacation rental properties are located in flat markets that do not have high rates of appreciation similar to residential markets.* Most rentals will sit for a longer period of time in comparison to residential markets. By "sit," I mean be prepared that your property may be listed for about one to two years.

I speak from experience. Remember, you are dealing with totally different markets here, and you may scoff when I mention some popular vacation areas as being "flat" when they appear to be the most highly coveted markets to vacationers. Keep in mind that even the most selective vacationer has their pick of the litter when buying a vacation home, especially when it is for personal use and they know they are going to have to carry these costs.

To get a better idea of how the market really is, get off your dock or take off your skis and look at the normal *residential properties* in the area and how they are performing. That is a much better indication of real estate in the region, as opposed to looking at other vacation rentals in comparison.

How about out-of-town investing and buying, sight unseen? I've done it before and I would do it again because now I have a system to allow me to move forward confidently. What we do now and what we would recommend to you is to carefully screen and select your team. In real estate, teamwork makes the dream work! In any area you are investing, you need to build a strong team—and the farther away you are from the region, the stronger your team needs to be.

Do NOT go straight away with the first professional you meet (as we often did). Commit to interviewing at least three professionals in each designated area (real estate agents, home inspectors, contractors, property managers) according to a specific set of guidelines and questions (see Appendix). This doesn't mean you can't go with the first person you meet, but it DOES give you more options, meaning you're doing your due diligence. If you cannot conduct these interviews in person, make sure to do so on video chat or some type of portal where you can see who you are speaking to, which will help you form a better judgment. And if you're not willing to drive or fly down to these areas before you get started, make sure to map out the entire area to find your bearings and give you a better indication of where and where *not* to invest.

Deciding what to invest in is also crucial so the agent knows *exactly* what you're looking for in terms of area, price point, and type of investment. When a property is found that meets your criteria, have your agent take a video of the place for you to view. Better yet, request a live stream so you can discuss details together. If it is something that you wish to put an offer in, the home inspector will provide a lengthy report to help you identify any deficiencies. Establish a list of things your agent should be on alert for as this will affect your decision-making process. Some common items would be mold, asbestos, plumbing, electrical, or structural problems (see Appendix).

Last but not least, work with a mortgage broker who is able to get you a mortgage in that area. Sometimes it's better to go local, as we did when we started in Northern Ontario. If you're renovating, make sure to notify your mortgage broker of your plans so they can get you the proper type of funding. This can help you leverage furthermore with *OPM*—other people's money—potentially saving you from using thousands of dollars out of your own pocket.

In hindsight, we learned that we could have used a Purchase Plus Improvements Program or a secured LOC to fund the $10K of repairs rather than paying out of pocket. That would have been a great use of OPM and we could have used that personal money to secure another property.

With the purchase of the third property, we also ran out of buying potential even though we still had money left to invest. We were not working with the same mortgage broker from the beginning who could provide us with a perspective of our overall financial situation and help us establish a plan to buy multiple properties without becoming over-leveraged. Instead, we were working with different mortgage brokers on a property-by-property basis. They had no idea of what we were looking to do as a whole, so were unable to see what our future buying power would be. They were only focused on getting us qualified for each individual property. So when we eventually tried moving onto property #4 and the banks refused, it was a huge shock and let down. Once again, I recommend working with a mortgage broker to help you establish a plan of action for exactly what you would like to do in your life, so this problem does not occur (see the Appendix for establishing your "*why*").

I will leave you with some closure. The Blue Mountain condo sat for two years on the market before it sold. We broke even. We still own the Timmins properties, both operating at an almost infinite return as the down payments required were so minimal in this market—and we have recouped our original investment through years of monthly cash flow of $400 per month (cash in pocket after ALL expenses including mortgage payments). The Timmins houses have both been cash cows that will fund two of our children's university education.

Chapter 4

Education Overload

With three properties under our belt, we were learning a lot from our experiences hands-on. However, we were already over-leveraged with three properties, meaning we couldn't qualify for any more real estate and we were almost out of money.

When you're over-leveraged it has to do with your debt service ratio. Lenders calculate the amount of debt that you carry and if it supersedes your income to the extent that the banks or a lender aren't comfortable with, it's highly unlikely you'll get financing. When this happened to us, we hadn't heard of it before, nor had we read about it in any of the real estate books we were reading. We needed to understand how to move forward.

We were beginning to recognize the need for a more systematic and methodological way of learning. Where does one seek education in real estate?

At the time we didn't know of any real estate investment courses, but we were given the advice time and time again that education is the #1 investment anyone can make. So when a free real estate information seminar appeared in our local paper, we jumped at the opportunity. We quickly secured a babysitter and made it our mission to attend.

When we arrived at the event it was a room filled with almost one hundred aspiring investors. We truly thought *all* the missing pieces would be found that night.

We sat near the front row as the presenter spoke about his WHY, combined with his real estate journey and what it helped him accomplish. We heard lots about goals, mainly family oriented. Aside from the showroom antics—such as free giveaways and action-takers railroading one another to make it to the front of the room to grab books, CDs, and $20 bills—we did learn a few valuable tips. However, it seemed as though the main premise of the presentation was aimed toward selling a $300 weekend course that would delve deeply into the topics that were briefly discussed that evening. I guess all the Neuro-Linguistic Programming (NLP) and sales tactics we experienced that evening worked. We obviously found something valuable about it as we found ourselves at the front of the line, signing up.

There was an intense gut feeling of *nagging doubt* and fear about losing my $300—similar to the fear of losing our $500 deposit for the block of land in Australia.

This fear continued overnight and into the next morning. It was so debilitating that it caused me to do more research and complete my due diligence about this course.

As I searched the name of the company online, a bunch of bad reviews popped up, but mainly a headline from an undercover story telling me what to expect on that three-day weekend: a series of what seemed like Neuro-Linguistic Programming (NLP) techniques to teach us the basics before promoting subsequent courses ranging from $40-$100K— along with extremely risky ways of paying for these courses (i.e., by credit). We also read a few horror stories about how guests are generally instructed to negotiate their credit limits during the course break, and open new lines of credit so they would be able to pay for these courses.

I was outraged that our $300 would probably not lead us to higher learning after all, but instead may be a prolonged sales pitch—leading me to phone the company directly and demand an explanation.

The woman on the other end of the phone seemed quite nonchalant as she explained we would learn things over the weekend, adding rather casually in there that we'd be presented with information about furthering our real estate education, and that they would be more than happy to give my $300 back if I changed my mind. This woman did not appear to be desperate or salesy, and left the final choice up to me—leaving me alone and confused about my decision.

I ended the conversation abrasively, stating something along the lines of, "I better learn something this weekend, or else!" and hung up. I braced my husband with the news that there was a chance we may not learn everything there is to know about real estate investing, even after we invest $300 and three days of our busy life. Despite this, we agreed to move forward with the three-day weekend as we were truly committed to learning how we could continue to build wealth through real estate.

Upon arrival for the three-day weekend course, we sat at a table with other participants, cluttering our space with notebooks and scribbling down every last word presented by the qualified trainer. And there were a LOT of words…"*why*'s," strategies, different presenters with different "*why*'s," and multiple investing tools. So we learned. We learned, and learned, and learned, and learned—until we were filling up a second notebook of information… and because there was so much information (almost like information overload) we only realized later, looking back, that there were what appeared to be different transitional sales tactics throughout the course (i.e., individualized meetings and one-on-one assessments, temperature control changes in the room, and very well-timed lunch breaks). We *learned* to the point that we felt we received our $300 worth.

Sure enough, we found ourselves in the hall upping our credit limits even after the trainer revealed it would be to pay for courses (I wonder if the lady on the phone line relayed our message?). But it felt natural to be doing this. We were told we were learning how to strengthen our negotiating skills and how easy it is to receive things if you simply ask. We really did feel like the money we were asking for was ours. That magical acronym again…OPM (other people's money). At the time it felt good.

Then…*the moment of truth*—we were finally presented with everything this weekend seemed to lead up to: additional courses to learn systems of each strategy we touched on over the weekend.

Our notebooks were full; however, they were filled with *half-complete strategies* used to build wealth in real estate. For instance, a page of my notebook reveals an investment strategy that was filled with the first five steps, but missing the remaining five that we learned later are essential in the formula. Stopping at that point would be like eating a sandwich without the filling, or baking muffins without the eggs and flour…like eating a Big Mac without the secret sauce. Really great, but highly unsatisfying—and who knows if it would really work?

We had *boatloads* of information, but no complete formula. No 100% proven step-by-step system. No *specific* recipe that clearly stated all the essential ingredients and instructions. We could see the value in upgrading our course, but the price tag—as well as the time commitment—was intimidating, to say the least.

Stopping at this point would basically put us right back to square one when we first sought out education. Lost, confused, and no proven system to move forward.

So my husband Vaughan and I reviewed our credit availability (which became ridiculously high because of our credit exercise during the break), as well as our calendar to see how we could squeeze in four courses and a mentorship into our schedules—all in between work and parenting three small children. *And we went for it!* We were committed down to the bone.

We ended up amongst a handful of others who also bought an upgraded, expensive course. Everyone else left with their notebooks. Whatever they did with that knowledge, we will never know—but as for us, our real journey began.

A payment was made on Sunday and our first online course began that Tuesday. Our three-day course was in June of that year. We completed four courses AND a mentorship by October. We were considered supersonic students, ripping through each course and applying all of our teachings as we learned. For us, the courses were fantastic! We learned the basic fundamentals of real estate, wholesaling, rent-to-own properties, and creative financing. Plus, we invested in a three-day private mentorship. We would learn a specific system for each strategy, and enjoyed the learning as well as the implementations and networking with likeminded people.

We attended the in-class component and were amazed when we discovered there were many people in the room amongst us who had paid the same price tag, but did *not* take action. Some signed up twelve months prior and were just taking their first course, or hadn't even invested in real estate yet. We thought this was the strangest thing: how can people afford to pay for this, and not use it?

We were frantic to pay off the $40-plus-K invested in our courses as we were suffering high monthly payments due to all the credit card debt we'd accumulated. Combine this strategy with the fantastic ways of using OPM (which the course instructors were classifying as the bank's money through more lines of credit, and more credit card debt)—

we were *drowning* despite the fact that we were actively implementing the strategies we learned to make a profit.

To make a profit, it took A LOT of work and it was not as simple as they made it sound in the three-day course. The first rule of thumb we learned in the upgraded course was that for every one hundred properties you look at, you will tie up about ten—and close on one. And that statistical rule pretty much applied for everything in real estate, business, and sales. *For every one hundred people you talk to...for every one hundred people you present an opportunity to...for every property you look at...*and so on.

In case you haven't realized this already, real estate investing takes TIME. A *lot* of time! So much time that we would NOT have been successful if I was NOT at home full-time working on this—at the *same time* as my husband was out all day at a full-time job paying the bills so we could support ourselves, our three children, and our growing credit card debt!

Many of the students in the course were working around the clock, and simply did not have the time and energy it takes to put into real estate investing. Even worse for some people: many would *quit* their job so they could claim their new title as a real estate investor before fully getting their hands dirty.

As an observer looking back in time, the whole process was seemingly filled with sales tactics and NLP techniques that really made us feel incredibly special, unique, and invincible. Some techniques were presented as if the "normal" rules in real estate didn't apply. Some basic things you should consider doing before taking other investors on your journey were skimmed over—such as funding partners, where investing experience is mandatory before you bring others on board. Even fundamental rules of thumb were only touched upon, such as retaining your full-time job so you can prove your income and qualify for mortgages. But not according to these trainers, who continuously stated that because we took a three-day course, we would be able to actively invest in these strategies and consistently be able to use other people's money, despite having little to zero hands-on experience. Talk about losing credibility and potentially losing your friends, never mind the possibility of a lawsuit.

More advice was given in the additional advanced courses we completed after our first four. Yes, we paid for more because we were learning. And we were effectively implementing the strategies we were taught.

But we soon understood that land development and commercial real estate are the most advanced types of real estate investing. Try learning on the fly with a one-hundred-unit apartment building! Or completing complicated deals like buying apartment buildings, strip malls, and land development...except in reality we were using *our* money to fund these courses, because at the end of the day you have to pay those creditors back.

All the sales tactics in the world could not lead me to believe that all of this was a good idea for everybody. Common sense tells you that *experience* is necessary to learn about investing, and that you should always learn on your own bill and NOT at the expense of others. It was also clear that a lot of people were somehow convinced they could spend thousands of dollars on these courses, despite the fact that many probably did not (and never would) have what it takes to be successful in this industry. To us it was very sad and daunting to witness what looked like vulnerable people being taken advantage of. In our perspective this made it quite clear that although valuable information and systems were taught, the #1 priority for these courses were not to help people, but simply to sell courses to anyone and everyone who would buy them.

Many also claimed that the strategies taught were unrealistic and ineffective in Canada. (Most courses offered to Canadian investors are American courses.) That, I would say, is not entirely true. The courses were taught by experienced trainers who were skilled investors and the strategies *did* work, however, students need to have time and the wherewithal to figure out what works and what doesn't, and combine classroom components with actual, *practical* learning.

As I stated in Todor Yordanov's book, *Real Estate: It's Not for You,* "Learning is doing." To experience real estate, you have to get your hands dirty.

Unless you partake in a joint-venture partnership or a six- to twelve-month mentorship (not three days) you will make mistakes, and you will lose money. And when you do, make sure it is your own, and does not belong to others.

We may have made a *lot* of mistakes—but I'm very grateful to not be writing about losing anyone else's money except for our own.

Education is *key* in real estate investing and you need to learn a *proven system* to be successful in the strategy you choose.

You can learn multiple strategies like we did, but it's best to pick *one* that suits your lifestyle (or desired lifestyle) and focus on THAT strategy.

If you are going to take a course, I would recommend investing in one that's based on real estate *fundamentals*. This is because good beginner courses are based on relatively the same basics, which will become the foundation of your learning. One of the only aspects that differs after this point are the trainers, the delivery, and the price tag.

There is no fault in investing a lot of money in your real estate education—but make sure you can afford it and pay for it properly, *not* on credit cards, or any way that will put you in an automatic deficit. Be aware of the numbers and what it will cost you per month when you use creative financing strategies for funding education and properties. Awareness is key and numbers never lie. It may feel like you aren't using your own money, but you are! And there are no sales strategies that can deny that.

When you are selecting courses and mentorships, ask yourself, "Can I really learn all there is to know in three days?" and, "What if I have a question after the three days are over?" or, "Are my trainers and mentors accessible to help me throughout the duration of our real estate journey, or do I need to learn everything in three days and figure it out by myself after the course is over?"

If I could do it all over again, I would not have paid as much money as we did. Instead, I would have taken advantage of local real estate networking groups to learn the basics of different types of investment strategies before paying for an expensive course. I also would have enrolled in a "fundamental" real estate investment course for a reasonable price that would not put me at a deficit.

And I certainly would NOT have funded our education on credit cards! My family and I silently suffered for years because of funding our journey on credit. This lifestyle created a pattern of living off a debt system, which I do NOT consider "*other people's money.*"

Soon after taking a real estate course that would teach the basics, I would then pick a strategy I wanted to specialize in and stick to that. I would do a joint-venture partnership where I would partner with an experienced investor—and shadow them as *they* manage the deal while *we* fund the investment, until I would know how to do this well enough to bring others on board...the true meaning of OPM.

The highest price or celebrity endorsement does not necessarily equal the best education. Shop around, use your judgment, and be highly aware of sales strategies—no matter how comfortable the room temperature is.

Chapter 5

Real Estate Rock Stars

If you have experienced NLP (Neuro-Linguistic Programming), you can relate to the fact that you may have a steep physiological response to certain statements that may be sales techniques (not always). Experienced NLP practitioners tend to elevate you out of your comfort zone, making you more likely to take positive action in different areas of your life. Invented by Richard Bandler and John Grinder in California, USA, NLP is a psychological approach to personal development, psychotherapy, and communication. Since the 1970s NLP claims a connection between neurological processes ("Neuro-"), language ("Linguistic") and human behavioral patterns learned and acquired through perspective and experience ("Programming"), and these can be altered to achieve life goals.

If you're unaware of NLP techniques and how they may be used, you might feel a slight feeling of elation or your heart palpitating slightly toward things you normally wouldn't care too much about.

When NLP is used in sales techniques, it may affect you and your decision-making process. In our real estate course, we became aware that trainers were using NLP to alter our mindset and sell their courses, which is quite normal and standard in any type of marketing and sales. But if you are not acutely aware of this phenomenon, you may not only be inclined to purchase programs and additional courses, but your entire perception of yourself and who you are may change.

All is fine and dandy until (at least for us) you combine it with a popular song by Nickelback (a famous Canadian rock group) about *"rock stars"*...

This song is a great example of how you might feel when you leave these types of courses: like a *rock star*. We were different. Special. Unique. We were "above" our friends and family. They didn't understand us (just like our trainers said they wouldn't) because we knew these "secret strategies." We were on the road to great wealth, and we had the spending habits to prove it.

Since we learned such unique strategies and were averaging $10K per deal on wholesaling, we were making great money—but because we were trained, in my opinion, *incorrectly* about OPM, *rather than paying money back* we became really good at charging our new, expensive lifestyle to our credit cards—and spending money twice as fast as it came in.

Gone was our noble goal of doing it all for our kids, supplementing income lost as I worked full-time, saving for their future. We were spending money like water. Private ski club memberships, golf club memberships, vacationing in luxury chalets in Blue Mountain and five-acre waterfront properties in popular getaway areas, celebrating our ten-year wedding anniversary (all six of us) at an Atlantis resort in the Bahamas AND marking the occasion, furthermore, with a 2-carat diamond eternity band happened all within the first six months of our real estate journey.

On the surface we appeared to be living like multimillionaires. On the outside we were like toy dolls, plastic and perfect. But looks can be very, *very* deceiving.

The deception went *way* beyond lifestyle. Our WHY—the very reason we took this leap into the unknown in the first place—was even more convoluted than our negative bank accounts and accumulating debt. Since we were official "FULL-TIME REAL ESTATE INVESTORS," we lived and breathed real estate, making real estate investing the new passion (and focal point) of our lives.

Let me take you back to the beginning. Remember my reasons for not working as a full-time teacher? How I was spreading myself way too thin and not giving work or family the 100% focus they deserve? Well, *work* certainly wasn't suffering as I was putting in twenty-hour days because I loved real estate *oh so much*. Our children were certainly getting the short end of the stick.

I was home (as in, working from home) but my mind and heart were in the real estate field. I used to call our kids our "junior business partners" because they joined us several times scouting properties, on construction sites for our development projects, and even joining us on business trips. Our daughter's first flight was to Timmins, Ontario, Canada, at four weeks old. Her first real estate investment meetings held by our club were *in utero*. For six months we were "the real estate group with a baby." The classic story of *dedication* is how I waived an epidural when I was in childbirth with her so I could use the fax machine as we negotiated a once-in-a-lifetime deal throughout the duration of my labor. I didn't have time to cook, clean, garden, or spend quality time with my kids, or with my husband. I was home, but I was not present or engaged with their lives.

But twenty-hour workdays meant that I was "dedicated to being a full-time real estate investor"—justifying my constant spending on our lavish lifestyle—until my *rock star* status came to a screeching halt, when a huge dose of reality slapped me in the face.

I cannot really admit any "would-haves" or "should-haves" as the absolute truth, but I can certainly admit that without any hindsight I wouldn't be who I am today—and I wouldn't be able to share these mistakes and lessons with you. As I look back on this particular time period, I can see this *rock star* multimillionaire mentality as our biggest downfall. In other words, our mental attitude was the #1 mistake we made, and the reason for our downward spiral. Because if we never spent money on a lavish lifestyle and instead continued to renovate and fund properties at a steady and controlled pace, we probably wouldn't have spun out of control.

NLP can be great! Look at Anthony Robbins. He uses NLP for *positive* purposes—to have you fight fears, motivate you, move you out of your comfort zone, and develop your true potential. *But NLP used in a negative way can be a set of completely different techniques,* and consumers should be well aware of what to look for before they, too, become "hypnotized."

NLP is used in almost all sales areas—even in shopping malls where they play upbeat music to get you in a shopping mood, or "trancy" music to make you feel important and hip. Another example is in casinos, where there are no windows and the temperature is extremely regulated to keep people awake, alert, and unaware of whether it is night or day.

When NLP is used in courses and seminars, be acutely aware of the way the trainers may treat you during the introduction, challenge your inner beliefs, and train you to say yes to almost everything to the point that you have agreed so many times that it's difficult to refuse any longer.

My eldest son played a trick on me that I would like you to try:

Say the word, "STOP."

Spell this word out loud four times.

What do you do at a green light?

Chances are, you will automatically say, "STOP!" even though the correct and obvious answer is "GO."

Now, this doesn't mean that we spent thousands of dollars on courses because we were hypnotized. However, if I could turn back time, I would have used the money we made in real estate to pay off the debt from our courses. I also probably wouldn't have fallen prey to my inflated ego as my new job title of "FULL-TIME REAL ESTATE INVESTOR." I would have created a balanced budget, with a surplus of income every month that would go toward purchasing ASSETS (items that put money *into* my pocket every month) as opposed to LIABILITIES (items that take money *out* of my pocket every month).

I would have focused on my status of "FULL-TIME MAMA" who creates income through real estate.

Most of all, I would've written down my "*why*" and displayed it in as many places as possible so I would never stray offtrack.

Today, I am not perfect. I am still a bit of a spendthrift (I probably always will be!). But in many cases I only pay cash. And I carry zero credit card debt. And I certainly do NOT use credit cards or lines of credit to fund our real estate transactions. Today, as experienced investors, we have found the true meaning of *no-money-down deals* where OPM comes from joint-venture partnerships with zero debt and win-win relationships.

Chapter 6

Jack of All Trades, Master of None

When you are doing EVERYTHING, you are often doing NOTHING. So I say now. *Rewind to twelve years ago...*

Although we started off with the buy-rent-hold strategy, after taking the expensive real estate courses we were applying each of their teachings not only for ourselves, but for others. We were practically doing EVERY real estate strategy for ourselves and for EVERYONE. We were flipping (and sometimes flopping!). Wholesaling and assigning. Buying and selling.

Preconstruction. Rent-to-owns (including five no-money-down deals!). Student rentals. Commercial and multi-family residential. Land flips and land development. Vacation properties. Mobile homes and mobile home parks. You name it, we've probably done it. And we were doing it for EVERYONE! If our business coach today, Joey Ragona, asked us, "Who is your avatar?" then our answer would probably be, "Anyone with a pulse." But even *that* criteria may be questionable.

At the time, we were priding ourselves on being able to help ANYONE with ANY type of real estate investment strategy. We were helping homeowners. People who were about to lose their homes, couldn't buy a home because of bad credit, or didn't want to use an agent to buy or sell their home. At the same time, we were working with investors (and often matching them with the homeowners). We believed EVERYONE should invest in real estate. The name of our company, Real Property Investments, has changed slogans more than Madonna over the years, originally starting out as, "Helping REAL People with Real Estate." If you wanted to invest, we could help even if you had NO money, NO job, and NO anything. And if you wanted to invest in an area we knew NOTHING about, we would become an expert in that area and find the perfect opportunity just for you! And we would.

Sounds great, doesn't it? For the investor, YES. For us, not so much. We were working twenty-hour days on a whim, meaning there was no structure. We were 120% *reactive* and had no predictability of what each day held. (On the plus side, I was a size 2.) I ALWAYS answered my phone and never had ANY idea WHO would be on the other end of the line (owner, tenant, or investor?), WHAT they would want (are we saving their house from foreclosure or are they an investor looking for a no-money-down deal?), WHERE they would want to invest (Toronto? Mississauga? Timbuktu?) and WHEN this transaction needed to be completed. More often than not we were dealing with crises that needed to be solved yesterday.

I was operating in crisis mode 24/7 with no control of my day whatsoever. I honestly thought this was a sign of success. The fact that we were EVERYTHING to EVERYONE, and I had a phone attached to my ear for twenty hours a day was a sign that we were "successful real estate investors." But the reality was much, much different.

We were hiding behind our busyness and we were drowning in debt rather than picking one strategy and focusing on it. When I did sleep, I would often wake up abruptly with night terrors, yelling and screaming. The time we spent with our kids was minimal as we were ALWAYS working.

I wouldn't admit to any of this until the night we met Joey Ragona, our business coach, at a Mastermind coaching session. Believe it or not, we were there to get new clients. And the only reason I went in the "hot seat" was so everyone could hear all about ME and what an accomplished investor I was...a plug for Real Property Investments! Boy, was I wrong. Joey hit all of our pain points and stopped us right in our tracks. He actually mapped out my entire day, hour by hour, documenting my so-called "busyness" and it was PATHETIC.

Looking at our lives, I could see hours of doing a lot of NOTHING albeit for chasing dead leads, hitting brick walls, and spinning my wheels. Most importantly, I realized how this lack of focus was making us miss the most important thing...our life!

Looking back, I can see we had a serious case of shiny object syndrome. We started off great with our buy-rent-hold strategy, but the more we learned and the more people we met and saw what they were doing, the more distracted we got. We can now see that you should pick one strategy that suits your lifestyle and learn everything about that strategy BEFORE implementing any others. Flip to the Appendix for a strategy on how to do this yourself.

It's okay to change strategies, but it's best to focus on only one at a time. Today, we focus on buy-rent-holds in specific areas and have developed a specific model in each area. We also form a team in each area that handle all operations involved in the transaction, freeing up a lot of our time.

We also stopped serving EVERYONE. Today we have a very specific avatar: investors who are pre-qualified and wanting to buy our specific model in the areas we invest in. We do not spend our days scouring for investors and investment opportunities. Instead, we analyze areas with strong economic fundamentals and formulate an investment model in that area (what type of property, price point and rental income are required) to give investors the best ROI from a cash flow and appreciation standpoint, while educating investors on these specific models in each area.

No more serving everyone everywhere. No more taking unsolicited calls. In fact, today I am only on the phone at scheduled times and I know exactly who I am speaking with (and what we'll be speaking about) so I am 100% focused.

True—the jittery excitement is no longer there, like it used to be. And the adrenaline has worn off, so I need to use some of my newfound time to exercise as my size 2 wardrobe is long gone. But today I can spend time on the phone catching up with friends. Spontaneity arises and is welcomed from our kids' unpredictable school and sports schedules. Our excitement comes from family travel, social gatherings with friends (no business talk), date nights, and, of course, cheering our kids on from the sidelines at all their activities... leaving our phones at home!

Chapter 7

Flip or Flop

Ahhhhh...house flipping!

If there's anything more exciting (and familiar) in real estate, that's flipping a house. On almost every channel you turn on television there seems to be an extraordinarily good-looking person who has the wherewithal to find a property in a prime neighborhood for pennies on the dollar, fix it up, and make oodles of cash! Easy money, right? Not so much!

But when we found two homes on a single lot listed for $35K—with the fair market value on each home being much, much higher—we thought we'd found a winner. These houses were located in Timmins and would be another addition to our investment portfolio. We knew $35K would likely be a phenomenal deal for both houses on one plot of land, regardless of the condition of the property. Each house faced on a major street and backed onto one another, allowing the possibility of a severance and *two* separate sales!

The property was located on Elm Street...and as this project was underway, we started referring to it as, "The Nightmare on Elm Street."

Mistake #1 was HOW we financed the property. Due to the low purchase price and our inability to qualify for another mortgage (or so we thought) we obtained a loan from a private lender to buy the property AND fund any necessary repairs, using our primary residence as security against the loan.

In flips, time is money—especially when you are paying 12% interest to a private lender! We were paying 12% interest every month. The idea was that after all was said and done, we would have MORE than enough money to pay off the private lender and ALL the credit cards, PLUS the mountain of debt we used to pay for our expensive courses and other real estate. Right? WRONG AGAIN!

Upon inspection of the property, our agent, who acted as our eyes and ears, reported his findings with the front house being small and simple with a full basement. But it was occupied by a hoarder, so it was difficult to see the condition of anything inside because boxes of stuff were piled up from floor to ceiling. The back house was already stripped down to the studs, ready to be rebuilt!

With an extremely cluttered house next to an empty house, we waived the home inspection...*mistake #2.* Instead of getting a home inspection, we had our contractor (managed by our property manager) view the property and go through a general checklist of what needed to be done, which helped us conclude our initial budget. We even flew to Timmins with a newborn in the baby carrier and saw exactly what they saw—initially confirming our checklist.

However, when the renovations began it was a different story. "There are mushrooms under your floor," was the first unexpected statement that led to a stream of other unexpected statements...that perhaps a home inspection could have helped avoid, or maybe not.

One of the worst parts of this flip was when an exterior pipe burst in one of the houses and threatened to flood the neighbor's home!

On top of that, as the hoarder's boxes were cleared, many left for us to dispose, this extra dump cost along with further unexpected costs continued to pop up.

But nothing prepared us for when our contractor decided to subcontract this job, whether knowingly or unknowingly, to less experienced workers who were producing amateur work that could have been done myself. Fortunately, our project manager noticed this immediately and fired the contractor who confessed, and he accepted the fact that he would not be paid for his work. The project was then set at a standstill.

Mistake #3 would be our issue with the contractors. We only received one quote from a single contractor, so when we were able to secure another reputable contractor and resume the project, we had to redo the budget which became compromised.

Contractors are not always easy to find because they're usually busy with other projects. And when you need one in an emergency situation, they seem to be MUCH more expensive than you originally anticipated. Projected quotes received on a leisurely walk-through can be doubled, if not tripled. This made us reevaluate everything in the renovation.

We found ourselves stressing out over the simplest things, such as kitchen cupboards and showerheads. Never mind the last-minute recommendation to add exterior renovations to house #1 by adding vinyl siding around the entire home, as opposed to painting it as we'd originally planned. The budget was spinning out of control to the point that I lost all track of finances.

We also discovered that the possibility of severing the lot so each home could be sold separately was not possible as the properties each shared a watermain. No wonder both were sold together as one property. This reduced our profits substantially from the possibility of making two separate sales to selling a single-family home along with an additional home in its backyard. We did account for both scenarios, though. But the consumption of time and energy on the application and communications that followed could have been gratefully avoided if we knew otherwise.

...And this is why we called it, "The Nightmare on Elm Street."

The truth is, by the time we finished flipping this property, so much had spiraled out of control from purchase to sale. To this date, I can't honestly tell you from a financial standpoint how well or how poorly this flip went. We ended up selling this house for $155K. Our renovation budget was about $40K, leaving us with a giant profit of about

$75K. Our lawyer was impressed. Our realtor was impressed. Everyone thought we did so well. But did we?

All our profits were absorbed by our debt accumulated from this project, as well as our existing debt. It felt as though we didn't make any gains at all, aside from a ton of experience and relief to have the lien against our primary residence removed.

HINDSIGHT
20/20

It's clear to us now what we did wrong.

Mistake #1 was definitely our most costly mistake. The way you finance flips and manage your finances throughout the duration of your project can really make or break the outcome. Obtaining a private lender at 12% interest, which is pretty typical for a private lending cost, was significant as the monthly carrying costs were enormous and really ate into our budget.

I can now look back and see that we should have worked with a lender specializing in flips who could have loaned us the purchase and renovation funds at a much lower cost. This would have saved us thousands of dollars as well as hours of sleepless nights. Alternatively, we could have worked with a JV (joint-venture) partner to qualify for the mortgage and fund the repairs and split the proceeds with them. With the amount we could have saved in financing, there would have been more than enough to go around.

Mistake #2: ALWAYS get a home inspection. Even if you decide to tear up the entire house, get them to inspect the entire lot. They are trained to go through a very specific checklist, unlike contractors, and you will get an honest and unbiased opinion about the property. Any additional problems can possibly be identified—especially with plumbing and electrical, which are very expensive if upgrades are required. Mold can be another serious issue as it can spread behind the walls and throughout the entire house. And if asbestos or lead paint are detected, these issues need to be addressed (often at a big cost) before renovations are made, and these costs need to be allocated into the budget. A foundation inspection is also important to check if the structure is compromised in any way. And if water is seeping into the property, the cost can make the entire flip unworthwhile.

Home inspectors will also inspect the exterior grounds of the property, looking at soil quality and condition as well as the slope, which may cause deterioration of the foundation from water penetration and pooling. They'll also detect any carpenter ants or other types of vermin, or trees and plants on the grounds attracting other unwanted unknowns. Or, even worse, they can detect any roots growing into the property. All of these boring things are often overlooked by novice flippers who are excited with kitchen and bathroom renos (much more exciting) as well as by contractors. A home inspector will go through a lengthy list, making sure all items are accounted for. We have included a list in the Appendix for you to use on your next flip to make sure you've taken all possible repairs into account.

Mistake #3 was only receiving one quote from *a single* contractor. No matter how good your quote is or how valuable your relationship with your contractor is, always get at least three quotes from three *separate* contractors. The reason for this is that if the contractor walks off the job (as they often do) or you need to fire them mid-job (like we did), you at least have backup quotes from the other contractors (if they are available) and these quotes can be used as bargaining power, helping to prevent people from taking advantage of your time-sensitive situation and quoting way above the norm.

In addition to your inspections and financing the property in a more cost-effective way, staying on budget is *mandatory* and all costs should be determined prior, *preconstruction*. In addition to all of these costs, tack on a contingency fund of $25K. I know this number sounds huge, but after experiencing firsthand what can go wrong, and seeing how things can pop up unexpectedly with timeframes often lasting longer than expected, this contingency fund will help you flip and not *flop*.

Lastly, establish your timeframe to flip and make sure you can afford to *double* that timeframe. We thought our flip would be complete in three months. It took us six. This unplanned extension definitely bit into our budget. And although we made a lot of money in this flip and "The Nightmare on Elm Street" turned into a dream property, the experience held true to its name.

Chapter 8

Mistake by the Lake

There is nothing I love more (aside from skiing...) than spending my summers cottaging. Swimming in the lake, paddle boating, canoeing, water skiing, or even just sitting on the dock reading a book are all my favorite pastimes. This is when I feel the most peaceful and the most like myself. So when we were finishing up our luxurious ski season, it only felt natural to start planning our summer. And where do Canadian millionaires play from May to September? Muskoka!

I always dreamed of owning a waterfront cottage in Muskoka. Less than two hours from Toronto a natural paradise awaits with ancient rocks, crystal clear lakes, and the call of the loon. The area is considered one of the most prestigious cottage countries within the province of Ontario. We travelled there frequently in the summer, and I spent my childhood at various camps and cottages throughout the region. And since we were still in *rock star* mentality, I felt as though our next purchase would be waterfront land in Muskoka.

I continuously fooled myself by saying over and over again, "I just want a place where I can spend the summer swimming with my kids." I was kidding myself because this wasn't really true—although I really *did* want to enjoy this time with them, what I *really* wanted was the status of cottage ownership by spending our winters in Blue Mountain (ski country) and our summers in Muskoka (cottage country). To me, doing this would be proof that we had "*arrived*"...that we were successful.

After looking at several cottage properties, it appeared that waterfront land would be a more feasible option. So I searched and searched until I finally found five acres of land on a small lake in Huntsville (a ritzy region of Muskoka) that allowed motorized boating. The property had two separate entrances—or "driveways"—the first toward the water, with the other accessible by a laneway. The waterfront area was already cleared and had an outhouse, a fire pit area, a picnic table, and even a small bunk house! Everything else was surrounded by lush green forest.

Then, my *rockstar* mindset set in and I came up with what appeared to be an "amazing" idea. We would build a cottage on the portion of land that was accessible by the laneway, rent that out, and use the waterfront portion for ourselves so we could spend our summers "swimming with our kids." We would vacation for FREE! We'd turn our liability into an asset! Brilliant, right?

Actually, yes. It *was* brilliant—and it got *even more* brilliant when I found a 1,200-square-foot doublewide for sale for $10K! With a little touching up, this glorified trailer would be in rent-ready condition. The owner would even transport it onto our lot for us. And when I placed a teaser ad on Kijiji that read, "FOR RENT: HOUSE IN THE WOODS," there was a long list filled with people eager to pay $1,200 per month to live in our humble abode.

Shopping for a waterfront property in winter seemed to be a good idea at the time. After walking through knee-deep snow, the lake views looked gorgeous and the forest was so peaceful. But when we closed on the property and began development in the spring, it was a different story. We soon realized we committed a cardinal sin in real estate...

WE BOUGHT SWAMPLAND!

A large portion of the waterfront area was swampland and served as a gigantic breeding pool for mosquitoes. I'd heard tales about the black flies and bugs in Muskoka during May and June (guess I never vacationed there long enough), but I never knew how unbearable it really was. After our first site visit with the surveyor, with all four kids in tow, we were covered in bugs and bites. What I pictured as a glorious afternoon in the woods by the lake planning our project turned into a day of screaming, itching, and learning—setting the foundation for one of our biggest lessons in this area, "In Muskoka you are either on swamp or rock." Why did our amazing, fancy ex-Toronto agent in his red Corvette who sold us this property fail to mention this?

As the project planning began, I soon realized this job would be a lot more extensive than simply moving a house from the swampland, plunking it in the middle of the woods, and renting it out. That would be the fun part. The behind-the-scenes job, not so much.

First off, we discovered that dealing with the municipality and completing pages and pages of applications would be complicated and time consuming. Another major disappointment was that we wouldn't be able to sever the lot after all and sell the non-waterfront portion to pay off the lot. Although the agent warned us this may be a problem (yet, we had more than enough road frontage) the answer was a resounding "NO" for the frustrating reason of, "JUST BECAUSE."

If you think arguing helps, you need to realize that when dealing in country towns everyone can know everyone and an unspoken battle may exist between locals (them) vs. outsiders (us). Yes, this is often true. If you think the locals in a municipality that is peppered with vacationers appreciates you being there, you are probably very wrong. The reality is, living in these towns is different than cottaging, and the apparent resentfulness was evident for us while trying to work with the locals and asking them to help out. My advice is to tread very, VERY lightly if you're marching on this path, and try not to step on anyone's toes. And as you know, when you are managing people on a deadline no matter where you are, this can be very difficult.

We did end up filling out applications for permits and paperwork to move the house, and quickly realized our thorough budget was compromised almost from the start. I really had no idea about the costs of surveyors and site plans in this area. Clear cutting and grading also added up, along with bringing in hydro poles and naming our street... yes, the laneway was given a name because of us!

What we *really* weren't ready for was when the well was dug without consulting the project manager, and it was dug IN THE WRONG SPOT. *Talk about a $10K mistake.* And before any of you think, "Why would you pay this person?" recall what I just mentioned. In small towns, everyone pretty much knows everyone. Argue with this guy and the project would have probably come to a standstill. Who would we have gotten next? No guarantees.

So, we continued. Because of the new challenge with the well, the site plan needed to be changed as the septic system needed to be a specific distance from the well, which obviously was an extra expense because the placement of the house needed to be altered... but the workers continued to grate the area, place the gravel (never knew gravel was so expensive) and dig the cement pillars that the house would be placed on.

Finally, the big day came—and the new house arrived from its original location onto our lot. The cranes were ready to lift it onto the pillars of the firmly set foundation, and our project manager was there to oversee everything.

...And then something happened even worse than the well.
THEY PLACED THE HOUSE THE WRONG WAY!

The house that was supposed to be facing the forest and backing onto the trees was now facing the road and backing onto a septic bed.

Yes, our backyard was a septic bed! But the most shocking part was when I saw this alongside the project manager and he asked *ME,* "Why is your house facing this way? It should have been facing the other way."

How can you possibly respond to that? All I could do was get in my car and drive away to regain my composure before our building site could become a murder scene.

Soon I was ready to do what I do best...renovate!

I love decorating, and renovating on a budget is something I thoroughly enjoy (and I'm pretty good at it!). A little paint and flooring can go a long way to provide a nice, clean home for a great tenant.

The doublewide was GORGEOUS by my standards—very spacious with lots of light and high ceilings. This is what I always looked at because it allowed me to see past the 1970s decor. If we had left the home the way it was in its original shape and done some patching up, it would have been a fine site with a spacious, clean house ready for a tenant. But...no. I did something I never did before and would never do again.

I deviated from my original plan (simple cottage to rent out and vacation for free), and listened to my agent's suggestion of, "Why don't you glorify this doublewide to the nines and flip this property for a hundred K profit?" Perhaps it was a combination of fresh air and dollar signs, but we agreed.

Our budget for the interior repairs and upgrades soon quadrupled in comparison to what we had originally planned. *But who cares!* we thought, *because we were going to get a six-figure return! And all of these renovations would be done by a custom home builder who works for minimum wage!* Snort-laugh if you must, but this was a reference from the agent and we were still trying to do everything we could to save our pennies.

To our surprise, everything started off great. However, soon enough the project began to move very slow. *So slow* that we had to send up some of our contractors from Toronto to help out. The project continued at a snail-moving pace, and rumor had it our project manager was vacationing in the bush—so aside from the occasional photo report and a weekend visit from ourselves and our contractors, we really had no idea what was going on. Until, finally, our contractor from Toronto described the situation.

Our $10-an-hour contractor was making this job his full-time position as though he had no intention to finish anytime soon. This project started in May and was supposed to be completed by August, ready for the end of summer or early fall market when everyone starts looking.

September came, and our house was nowhere near done. We were out of time; and, more significantly, we were out of money.

The budget became *three times* the anticipated cost. We blew through all of our renovation money and were now back to using credit cards, adding more to our debt.

Our financial situation was dire and what originally began as a no-money-down deal ended up costing us thousands and thousands of dollars. Instead of a six-figure gain, we were looking at a six-figure loss.

The stress was immense and our pathetic story ended with firing the contractor and hiring two amazing friends and contractors from Toronto to finish the entire project in four days over the Thanksgiving long weekend. We were in October by this point. My husband was by their side helping, and no one came back to Toronto until the job was done and ready for the appraiser arriving that coming Tuesday.

What they accomplished over those four days was nothing short of amazing. There were no excuses, no breaks, nothing but work from 6:00 a.m. to, well, past midnight until the job was done.

Crisis averted, right? ...*Wrong!*

We listed the property and rather than selling instantaneously like we envisioned, it sat. We missed the important August/September deadline.

More significantly, we missed the newsflash that cottage markets are probably the *flattest* markets out there, no matter how much everyone desires the lakefront lifestyle. We had buyers browsing, but no one buying—the main reason being they wanted to have a view of the lake and not have a room backing onto a septic tank.

Eventually we managed to secure tenants. But since we listened to the agent's advice and over-improved the home, we were in financial distress. We were no longer able to implement our original, simple, yet strategic plan: rent out the cottage to cover our expenses and use the waterfront portion for ourselves and vacation for free.

Three agents and two years later our property finally sold...for a loss. We barely survived to tell our tale of our mistake by the lake.

Looking back on this tale of unfortunate events, I now realize there is so much we could have done differently.

Take cottages—or any second home that you intend to use—for what they are: *liabilities.*

A cottage is NOT an asset. It is a *liability* because it will take money out of your pocket every month.

Yes, people do rent out their cottages and can help carry these expenses, but we already discussed the challenges involved with this. The first lesson is if you buy a cottage for you and your family to enjoy during the summer months (mainly July and August in many places), make sure you're able to afford the cost of cottage ownership. Set aside a minimum of 5% for maintenance as they are money pits as well as tax burdens and full of expenses during the off-season when you are not even using the cottage.

In an ideal situation, own your cottage outright so you are not burdened with the stress of monthly mortgage payments that will continue during the off-season. Tally up all of these costs and then take out the family calendar from May to September and see how often you are really available to even use the cottage. You will be amazed how your vacation retreat can become a chore after commuting two hours each week in cottage traffic and you miss out on local happenings because you feel guilty if you are not using your cottage every weekend.

Some summers, we spend a week with family in Calabogie, Ontario; a week in Mont-Sainte-Anne, Québec; and a long weekend on Lake Muskoka, Canada. After looking at our summer calendar, this is all we can really fit in! And with plans to travel abroad, we would not have time to use the cottage at all.

It is always worthwhile to do the calculations of cottage ownership vs. renting a cottage during the weeks you are actually free to use it!

With the freedom of renting someone else's cottage, you also have flexibility with your area selection, time you're going, and the price—without any headaches of ownership! And don't underestimate the pleasures of visiting friends at their cottages.

Cottages are fantastic, but make sure you are not financially and emotionally bonded to the cottage in a way that removes the pleasure and it becomes a burden and obligation.

The second lesson to this story is *always stick to your original plan*! If we did not change our plan halfway through, we would probably own this property today mortgage-free. But I let a six-figure number and some vague ideas change our plans. Even though these numbers were backed up with research, the reality was our Plan B (holding the property) could not be comfortably supported.

The third lesson is the importance of staying on budget. Since this was our first development project, there were a lot of unexpected costs, despite the fact that I thought I did my homework by preparing an extensive checklist.

Your budget needs to be constantly monitored and reviewed. And just like with flips, you should have a contingency fund—but if you're building, you should add a denser layer of padding to that. In developments, BIG mistakes can happen and they are not optional to fix. Problems can be unforeseen and unpredictable, and funds need to be available to deal with these potential surprises.

Today, I always advise our investor clients—regardless of what strategy they are practicing in real estate—to ALWAYS BE PREPARED TO HOLD YOUR PROPERTY for a minimum of two years. I advise this so in case things go wrong (like it did for us), you are not left in a dangerous situation.

The final lesson I will leave you with is to *always be your own project manager* if you are doing an extensive flip or development. When the cat's away, the mice will play...and while our so-called "custom builder" could have been installing flooring and our kitchen, we were told he was busying himself by making custom crown moldings and playing Candy Crush Saga on his phone. The only time this project got completed was when my husband was on-site working and inspecting alongside the contractors.

Looking back, I probably should have either pitched a tent on-site, or rented a nearby cottage to visit the grounds every day and monitor all activity to make sure this flip stayed on a strict timeframe and budget. Because no one really cares about your project like you do.

If you are not watching your site every day, it's highly likely your contractors WILL play. Wells can be dug in the wrong spot. And project managers can go on vacation mid-project. You can hire all the people in the world, but at the end of the day, 100% of the responsibility is yours!

Chapter 9

Rock Bottom

Rock bottom is a very interesting place to be.
Imagine all your greatest fears and unknowns you've been dreading and would do anything to avoid, and then be with them and walk amongst them. Days blend into months and into years as you walk around in this haze struggling to get through, fighting a series of constant battles and peppering yourself with positivity to go toward the only direction possible...up.

The emotions that can constantly accompany you are anxiety, depression, and restlessness. No matter what you're doing, whether it's enjoying time with friends and family or doing something you love, you're preoccupied with your situation, leaving you saucer-eyed and looking like a person on the edge. I have seen this look in the eyes of several real estate investors and entrepreneurs over the years and it is NOT the look of freedom or someone who is achieving their "*why*."

We were holding two negative cash-flowing properties we were desperately trying to sell (Blue Mountain and Muskoka), along with our outstanding debts from LOCs and credit cards—*totaling six figures*—some as high as 25% interest.

Our monthly carrying costs to pay private mortgage payments and the minimum for credit cards was over $6K per month.

This was on top of our normal cost of living.

I spent hours a day, every day, paying bills the only way I knew how...borrowing from Peter to pay Paul. This was a skill I learned to perfect (and not a good one) as borrowing from borrowed money does not solve this problem but leads to a perpetuity of debt.

Through this experience I learned how to befriend instead of fear debt collectors. I learned what happens if you do not pay your bills on time (practically nothing). I learned how to live in constant overdraft. And I became very familiar with the three dreaded letters—NSF—appearing on my bank statement every month to the point that my monthly bank charges totaled the cost of a mortgage payment. But at the end of the day, everyone got paid. Maybe not in full and maybe not on time, but at least for our credit to remain intact to maintain a healthy score that we worked on increasing.

Even more dire was our accounting situation. Our real estate course trainers advised us to incorporate, but somehow we ended up with three years' worth of *unfiled* tax returns in three separate corporations. *That is a total of nine overdue tax returns!* Because we were doing so many different types of real estate strategies and buying so many different types of properties, our paperwork was a total fiasco and beyond the stated capabilities of Turbo Tax or H&R Block. We started out with our regular accountant who filed our taxes like he always did, which we later found out was quite aggressive (he tried to deduct the entire amount of our courses in one year!). This resulted in a very stressful audit and taking our situation to another accountant to help us out. The second accountant had been through the same training as we had, so we thought she'd be perfect to help us out. She even introduced us to a bookkeeper to help us get all the entries done properly.

At the time I knew very little about accounting or QuickBooks and I was certainly *not* organized. Under the spell of taking the real estate courses, I actually said I needed to outsource someone to do these types of linear and methodological items "because I am an entrepreneur and it hinders my creative thinking."

So I was looking forward to handing over years of paperwork to someone who was expected to magically organize and input everything and submit it to our accountant.

This situation dragged out for years. The bookkeeper could not make sense of much of the information provided, and in her defense, no one (including myself) really could. This job included translating BOXES of paperwork. I may not have been filing throughout the years, but I was certainly printing! And remember how active we were, averaging five to ten real estate deals per month for our investor clients? Think about the paperwork that results from one deal alone and multiply that by ten. *Then* divide it amongst three separate corporations...four, considering some were included in our personal name. And because of this mess, we had to include the personal files of a working dad and self-employed mom and the life of four kids! Total circus!

Our accountant's work was understandably slow, but her bills were steady. Accountant #2 was amazing at getting us through our audit triggered from accountant #1, but then became unresponsive and mysteriously disappeared due to which we later found out as health problems. We were then introduced to accountant #3, who not only advised us on how unnecessary it was to have three corporations, but also informed us that the previous accountant was advising the bookkeeper on incorrect submissions—making us start all over.

Bills kept coming, along with drip-fed results that were more often incorrect than not... making us realize it was finally time to let the previous bookkeeper go. Accountant #3 was left to make sense of her apparently nonsensical entries, which resulted in a huge bill. Without the slightest amount of over-exaggeration, the final tally of combined fees from our bookkeepers and accountants over this extensive period was $40,000.

The good news is that Mama (me) didn't have to go to the pen for unfiled tax returns. Topically, it was our financial situation that made us feel like we were at rock bottom. But once we got to the bottom of our outstanding bills, we would see it was more...much more!

From a personal standpoint, we were consumed with our financial situation and neglecting our *"why"*—our family. Working to tackle this debt was all we did. We spent next to zero time with our kids and zero time with each other unless we were working. We would chauffeur our children to all of their extracurricular activities and attend their school events; however, instead of embracing these moments and cheering them on, we would be on the sidelines with our heads buried in our phones, texting or taking calls. And when we were watching, we would see right through them as our thoughts would be on how to fix our crisis of the day and how the hell we were going to get out of the situation.

Destructive thoughts haunted us and followed us throughout all daily activities, including networking events and dinner parties. It only turned into conversations between my husband and I when we discussed our situation every night until it carried into our dreams, resulting in a routine of night terrors and consistently dreading sleep. Nighttime was the time my unconscious mind ran rampant and I was not awake to reassure myself that we could get through this and that everything would be okay. Every night, without fail, I would wake up terrified, yelling and screaming and cowering in the corner afraid to go back to sleep.

In spite of our personal and financial suffering, I was still under the false notion that this was part of our real estate investment journey and was typical of the daily struggle experienced by any entrepreneur with a business startup. We survived with the idea that we had to persevere and engage in this never-ending daily grind—*because if we weren't working, we weren't achieving.* This perverse and demented belief led to me working twenty-hour days building our business while simultaneously tackling our financial problems and going through the daily routines of motherhood.

I thought I was doing it all (entrepreneur, investor, full-time mom) and truly believed we were on the road to success. But, in reality, we were on the road to nowhere.

HINDSIGHT
20/20

When you begin investing in real estate, *you need to treat it like a business.* Although you need to stay open and creative like an entrepreneur, you simultaneously must be organized and methodological with a strategic business plan in place.

Part of setting up your real estate investment portfolio like a business entails starting with the end goal in mind. We opened up three corporations because that is what we were *told* to do when we studied our real estate courses. Not only did this result in a huge expense, but it was also unnecessary. Before doing anything, meet with a tax professional—or perhaps more than one—tell them your goals, and consider their professional opinion. Many will recommend doing everything in your personal name, saying it is unnecessary to incorporate. From our experience, I regret buying any income property in our personal name as it results in a lot of extra bookkeeping and accounting and I strongly believe in separating business from personal. On the other hand, three corporations (for us, at least) was total overkill and led to increased paperwork, as well as insane accounting expenses.

It's also important to have a strategic filing system to organize all paperwork for business transactions AND banking transactions. *Even if you outsource bookkeeping and accounting, you need to keep track of your own records and should be able to retrieve any piece of information from your desktop in as little as thirty seconds.* You should be able to hand over all of your records to your bookkeeper and accountant, or even input the entries yourself in a clear and concise manner, which will keep your accounting costs down and allow your filings to be completed on time. It also allows your accountant to focus on what they should be focusing on—to help you track your wealth and minimize your taxes so you can move forward with a successful real estate investment portfolio and wealth building plan.

Chapter 10

Rising Up

Despite us being in a constant state of distress, we were generating active income from our real estate business which is based on helping other investors grow their money in real estate the *correct* way. More importantly, we were focusing on helping our investor clients avoid the mistakes we made. Back then it was a classic case of, "Do as I say, not what I do."

While all hell was breaking loose, we continued to look for undervalued and no-money-down deals, helping others become successful in real estate by assigning these lucrative opportunities to other investors for a fee of $10K-plus per property. Our main source of income was generated by wholesaling and assigning properties. This helped us pay our extravagant debt and living expenses. We started doing this after the completion of our wholesaling course early on in this adventure and became extremely good at it. Our first assignment was a 5-plex we secured in Northern Ontario for $55K with the appraised value of $110K and an after-repair value of $210K. We even secured grant money to pay for all improvements. We were expanding in new areas based on research of economic fundamentals and forming teams in each area to help find undervalued properties.

We also had steady income from our cash-flowing rental properties; our $40K single-family homes in Timmins, Ontario. If it wasn't for this income, bankruptcy would have been inevitable.

The reality of our situation weighed on me very heavily. It was more than emotionally exhausting as we continued to plough through the days, living and breathing real estate and ignoring life all around us consumed by the all-encompassing debt.

...Until one night we found ourselves at a coaching "Mastermind" session led by business coach Joey Ragona. We weren't there to discover what we did *not* know, but instead to proudly proclaim what we DID know to the other investors in the room! *A built-in audience of sitting ducks forced to listen to what I had to say about real estate!* I anxiously thought. We were supposed to talk about how great we were and how we managed to "do it all." At least that was our intention, until Joey put me on the hot seat and we left the coaching session realizing that we knew...NOTHING!

Naked. Vulnerable. Exposed. That is how it felt to be stripped of the notions that we were "living the dream" as full-time parents AND real estate investors; that our so-called "insane busy schedule" (that no one in the world but supersonic me could handle) is not so busy after all, but instead a sequence of unproductive tasks mustered together to create the illusion of busyness.

We were stripped of my unwavering proclamation that I shouted from the rooftops for the previous five years, "*My passion is REAL ESTATE.*"

Fortunately, my reaction to this revelation was NOT to retreat and continue with these old beliefs, but to reach out to Joey and ask for help. He graciously accepted and our coaching journey began.

Or so we thought.

Our first meeting was alone with Joey to discuss our twelve-month goals. We focused on systemizing our business, creating multiple streams of income, and amplifying our portfolio.

Although Joey was supportive and respected our topical goals, he gently identified the underlying issues that needed to be cleaned up first. He pointed out what we were avoiding and what kept dragging us under. We spent the next several months dealing with three years of unfiled taxes and incomplete bookkeeping. I was even trained to do the bookkeeping myself on QuickBooks and learned how to organize everything using a wonderful program called "*Accountant-In-A-Box.*" This program taught us several simple, yet valuable strategies to organize our financial information and know exactly where we stood financially. This program was so straightforward. Soon after dedicating a couple of hours per month to bookkeeping, we no longer required the services of a bookkeeper.

Through Mastermind sessions and personal coaching with Joey, we worked through our personal feelings and fears that were subconsciously attaching us to our cash-sucking properties that would not sell, draining us of our hard-earned income. Robert Herjavec from the *Dragon's Den* TV series refers to stopping these type of cash drains as, "Stopping the bleeding." Once the emotions become identified (ego, fear of failure, personal attachment) we were finally able to "break up" with these properties and focus on aggressive sales tactics until they were eventually sold, saving us thousands of dollars every month.

We took any recovered income and focused on tackling our huge debt. Joey forced us to actually identify our debt, which was so overwhelmingly scary. We had to list it on a spreadsheet so we could see *exactly* what we were up against.

After the initial shock wore off, we reviewed various strategies in which we could *kill* the giant.

But even putting down large sums against this debt could be described as throwing pebbles at a giant. I wanted to win this battle more than anything, but because of our debt and the way we looked on paper (one salary with ownership of multiple properties and a six-figure debt load), refinancing our personal residence was not even an option at this time until a significant amount of debt was paid off.

We focused on accounting, getting our finances in order, and debt reduction for over a year and a half through strategic goal setting and planning set out in daily, ninety-day, and yearly coaching sessions. And would you believe in addition to living off of one steady paycheck, operating an expensive business, and raising four growing children, *we managed to make it happen.*

We paid off enough of our debt—over $100K—so we were able to refinance our house and pay off all remaining debts.

From a financial standpoint we were back to where we started *before* we began investing in real estate.

The big difference today is that we are armed with the knowledge and firsthand experience to successfully move forward...and achieve all of our dreams!

Chapter 11

The True Meaning of Success

Out of all the lessons we've ever learned, we have noted some of the most important takeaways while getting our finances in order. Now we pass them onto you.

- **Having your kids home and ignoring them for work is NOT spending quality time with family.**
- **Going out to work events with your spouse is NOT the same as actually spending time with them, i.e., on a date night.**
- **Neglecting your personal growth and enjoyment is NOT necessary to become successful. Stop putting yourself last!**

In short, Joey Ragona taught us how to have our life back!

Through self-identification, awareness, and support, Vaughan and I now have a revamped schedule. 80% of my time is devoted to being a wife and a mother, while 20% is dedicated to our business even though we are bringing in four times the income through organization and prioritization.

We have since developed systems that have increased our income FIVE TIMES MORE PER YEAR. In many ways, this is only the beginning.

I no longer have a phone growing out of the side of my head.

Today, I am rarely on the phone aside from pre-set appointments on certain days of the week during very specific hours. In fact, my phone is often turned off so I can be engaged with the world around me; with the life that we are creating for and with our family.

Rather than working on the sidelines of the kids' sports, we are now on the field with them coaching their teams. We are in their classrooms volunteering and spending free time together as a family watching movies, going to the park, or traveling the world.

We frequently spend quality time as a couple. We jog together every morning surrounded by nature and go downhill skiing in the winter. We dine out at new restaurants with other couples and friends. We attend personal growth workshops. And...we are even trying new sports, like golf and curling!

With our heads out of the sand with our business, and instead having a clear vision with one another, our marriage has reached new heights and increased our productivity as business partners.

We are finally being authentic to our WHY. It may have been a difficult road to travel, but looking back I wouldn't have it any other way.

And I will leave you with these final words of advice...

- **Be true to your WHY.**
- **Stay financially balanced as much as possible.**
- **Choose an investment strategy and build an investment portfolio that fits WITH your life, not FIGHTS with your life (a wonderful quote from our dear friend Gillian Irving).**

Most importantly...*live your BEST life!*

Appendix

SPECIFIC GOALS: Moving Past Fears and Finding Your WHY

© Joey Ragona

WHY ARE YOU INVESTING IN REAL ESTATE?

The big "WHY" is always a topic of discussion at real estate events and workshops.
And, for the most part, people usually use a top, surface level want as their "*why.*"
Example: "*I want to make five thousand dollars of monthly cash flow so I can replace my income and quit my job.*"
Good start.
But in my experience, "quitting my job" is NOT the real "*why.*"

Here's How You Find Your Real Why:

Please don't be fooled by the simplicity of this exercise. I do this constantly in my coaching. I have followed this formula forever and it always gets to the DEEPEST roots of what's important.
Ask yourself, "*Why is that important?*" at LEAST FIVE times.

Here's How This Works:

Why do I want to invest in real estate?
Because I want to replace my income.
Why is that important?
I want to quit my job.
Why?
Because I don't like getting up at 6:00 a.m. every morning, driving for an hour in the morning and at night, and then doing it all over again the next day.
Why?
I'm not seeing my kids enough.
Why is that important?
Because when I get home, I'm cranky and just want to crash because I'm so tired.
*We could dig deeper here...*but for the sake of time and space, we have now discovered the REAL reason for this dude to invest in real estate is NOT for the five thousand a

month or quitting his job.

The real reason is so he can stay home and be with his kids while they grow up, and not missing out on those precious years.

Here's How You Keep Motivated:

WRITE YOUR GOALS DOWN.

Simple.

Yet few people do this.

I was one of them.

Until I realized that all of the richest people in the world write down their goals, READ THEM every day, and stay accountable to reaching those goals.

Listen—I'll be the first to tell you, more than likely, you will NOT reach some of your goals immediately.

It's simply because you have to adjust the way you do things or get more information (whatever it is).

And that's PERFECTLY normal.

But here's the *GOOD NEWS*.

YOU'RE ACTUALLY DOING SOMETHING AND MOVING FORWARD...

Even if you don't reach your goals in the time frame you set.

That's life. It's business.

But you'll be so different from people who sit in seminars, do NOT write down goals, and keep themselves accountable.

Those people are dreamers. Not doers.

Doers make mistakes. But doers are moving forward.

If you're scared of making mistakes...don't move forward—it's that easy.

But you'll be a part of the "dreamers" statistic.

And that's something we want to help you avoid at all costs!

Screening Questions for Your Real Estate Professionals

Commit to interviewing at least three professionals in each designated area—including real estate agents, home inspectors, contractors, property managers—according to a specific set of guidelines and questions.

© Monika and Vaughan Jazyk

QUESTIONS FOR REAL ESTATE AGENTS

1. How long have you been in the real estate business?
Ideal time is three to five years.

2. Do you work with real estate investors? If so, how many?
You want a real estate agent who has experience working with investors, but at the same time you do not want them to have too many because YOU want to be a priority.

3. Do you specialize in any type of real estate, or any particular area? What areas of town are appreciating? What areas are rents increasing?
Your real estate agent should be familiar with the overall market in their area and surrounding area; however, they should also be experts in specific areas and specific types of investment properties.

4. Do you depend on real estate to make a living?
If your real estate agent sells real estate as a side gig or past time, our recommendation is to find a new agent who lives and breathes real estate. Your goal is to work with agents who depend on real estate to make a living so they will make you a #1 priority.

5. Are you willing to put the time in to find me the right property? How much time do you have?
Investors are high-maintenance and require the agents to view multiple properties before they put in an offer. Make sure the agent has the time and patience for this, otherwise they will likely get fed up and stop working with you.

6. Do you have any banking or funding connections?
Quite often, real estate agents work closely with mortgage brokers and private lenders. Being familiar with different financing criteria can open up opportunities for creative financing strategies, if needed.

7. Do you own any real estate? Are you an investor? Do you live in this area? Is most of your real estate activity focused in this area?

Ideally you will want a real estate agent who LIVES, WORKS and INVESTS in that particular area because that makes them an *expert* in that area. They should always be up to date with happenings in the area from a resident, professional, and investor standpoint.

8. How many properties do you currently have listed?

Ideally the answer is a very low number. If they have numerous properties listed that means they are probably not selling. You want to work with *selling* agents, not listing agents!

9. How many properties did you sell last year?

An active agent will be buying/selling three to four properties per month. The average real estate agent sells only three to four properties per *year*! Chances are the more active the agent, the better your results.

10. Can you provide five references?

Make sure to call these references (yes, pick up the phone and call them or meet in person to get a gut feeling) to verify the agent's work ethic, performance, credibility, and overall attitude.

QUESTIONS FOR PROPERTY MANAGERS

1. What types of services do you provide?

Find out if they provide full-service or à-la-carte property management.

2. What are your charges for your services?

Do they charge a percentage of rent each month? Or are there extra charges?

3. What types of services will you contract out? Do you receive discounted rates for these services? Are you receiving competitive quotes?

Contractors, tradespeople, cleaners, etc. should be competitively priced and well screened. The property management company needs to do their due diligence. You always have the right to find your own workers, as well.

4. Will you provide monthly revenue and expense statements?

Financials should be provided monthly in a clear and accurate manner allowing you to easily transfer the information to your accountant at tax time.

5. What method and date each month will we receive our rental income?

How will they distribute rents to you every month? E-transfer? Direct deposit? Will it be on the first or the fifteenth (property management companies sometimes do this to give them time to collect late rent from tenants).

6. How will you communicate with us regarding the status of each unit?

Communication is key. A good property manager will update you on tenants, repairs, and maintenance of the property and inform you of happenings every month. They will also notify you of upcoming repairs and maintenance so you can budget accordingly.

7. Do you handle paralegal matters such as serving tenants and going to court if necessary?

This is key. If not, you need a paralegal—preferably one that communicates and works directly with the property manager.

8. What is your experience and knowledge base of the Ontario Landlord and Tenant Board (or the tenant board or governing body in your province/state/country)?

Ideally your property manager needs to be familiar with the current tenant and property laws and educate themselves on an ongoing basis in regards to any policy changes.

9. Are you a licensed property management company?

10. Do you carry insurance? If so, what kind?

11. Do you have a manual outlining all of your services and policies?

12. How many units are you currently managing?

You want to know this to find out if they have enough time for you!

13. Can you please provide five references?

Make sure to get addresses so you can drive by the actual properties. See if you can view any properties they are currently managing.

QUESTIONS FOR HOME INSPECTORS

1. How long have you specifically been in the home inspection business?

Your goal with this question is to gain insight into their specific home inspection experience. What you need to determine is how many years of actual full-time home inspection experience the individual may have.

2. How many home inspections have you personally completed?

The more, the better. Make sure it was completed by them as an individual and not their *firm* (or company) overall.

3. What is your work background?

A construction background is always preferred.

4. What qualifications do you have?

Although home inspectors are not required to be qualified, it is always best to use someone who is a "National Home Inspector" (NHI) or equivalent.

5. What types of reports do you provide, and how long after the inspection are they received?

Reports should be detailed, easy to follow, and accompanied by photos. Ideally, reports are available twenty-four hours after the inspection.

6. How long is the average inspection?

A typical pre-purchase inspection of an average size home of 1800-2500 sq. ft. should usually take two to three hours (dependent on property age and condition). Longer is not necessarily better or required, but an extremely short inspection of an hour or a quick walk-through should be cause for concern.

7. May I attend the inspection?

You should always be invited to attend a home inspection.

8. Can you provide approximate costs for repairs and improvements?

They can, but they are not allowed to subcontract work for you or be affiliated with contractors (part of their code of ethics). All quotes are considered a jumping-off point and you would preferably be encouraged to receive written quotes from independent contractors.

9. Can I call at a later date for information or advice?

You should always be able to contact the inspector after reviewing the report.

10. Can you provide five references?

Pre-Purchase Checklist for Home Inspector

Establish a list of things your agent and home inspector should be on alert for as this will affect your decision-making process. Some common items would be mold, asbestos, plumbing, electrical, or structural problems.

© Monika and Vaughan Jazyk

Inspection Date:

Property Address:

Property Description:

☐ Single

☐ Double/Duplex

☐ Triplex

☐ Multi-Unit

☐ Unfurnished

☐ Furnished

Other Property Particulars:

Examine Exterior of Home

1. Foundation

☐ Type of foundation:

☐ Condition (missing mortar in joints/open holes/cracks/other/damage)
Comments:

2. Roof

☐ Type of roof:

☐ Shingles (missing pieces/cracking, damage)

☐ Framing (bowed sheathing/sagging ridge)
Comments:

3. Windows

☐ Type of windows:

☐ Condition (caulking needed/broken glass/missing putty/missing latches)
Comments:

4. Roof Vents

☐ Flashing (defective/needs repair/leaking)

☐ Condition (broken/damaged/missing)
Comments:

5. Grade

- ☐ Does surface water flow toward house/building?
- ☐ Location of dry walls (yes/no)
- ☐ Possibility of flooding (yes/no)

  Comments:

6. Mechanical Systems

A) Heating

- ☐ Type:
- ☐ Condition (functions/needs repairs)
- ☐ Type of fuel used (oil/gas)
- ☐ Firestopping needed (yes/no)
- ☐ Safety valves and shutoffs work properly (yes/no)
- ☐ Sufficient heat is produced (yes/no)
- ☐ Number of zones (1/2/3)
- ☐ Needs servicing or cleaning (yes/no)

  Comments:

B) Plumbing

- ☐ Drainage (poor/fair/good)
- ☐ Water pressure (adequate/inadequate)
- ☐ Leaks (yes/no)
- ☐ Septic or cesspool system works properly (yes/no)
- ☐ Use of lead water lines or lead traps (yes/no)
- ☐ Sufficient amount of shutoff valves (yes/no)
- ☐ Shutoff valves working (yes/no)

  Comments:

C) Electrical

- ☐ How many amps (60/100/150/200)
- ☐ Main disconnect working (yes/no)
- ☐ Serviced, grounded (yes/no)
- ☐ Use of (lamp cord/knob and tube wiring)
- ☐ Aluminum wiring (yes/no)
    Comments:

Basement Interior

1. Water Penetration

- ☐ Location:
- ☐ Efflorescence (yes/no)
- ☐ Sump pump working (yes/no)
    Comments:

2. Cellar Floor

- ☐ Condition (holes/evidence of water/cracks/needs repair)
    Comments:

3. Foundation Walls

- ☐ Accessible/Inaccessible
- ☐ Condition (poor/fair/good)
    Comments:

Contractor Questions

Fundamental questions you should always ask your contractor before getting involved.
© Monika and Vaughan Jazyk

1. Are you licensed, bonded, and insured?

2. What areas have you worked in?

3. Describe your team. How many contractors per project? Who are your specialists, such as the electrician and plumber?

4. Do you have a good relationship with suppliers for materials, and are you able to get discount builders' prices? Do you have accounts in which you can defer payments?

5. Provide ten references we can contact for recent jobs.

Property Assessment: Best Stratetgy to Find the Right Property

© Joey Ragona

To help you decide which real estate model is best for you, I've created a short exercise that I use with all of my coaching clients.

One of the biggest obstacles for people to get started investing in real estate is knowing for themselves, "Which model is right?"

I've heard that question over and over again and the answer is, in my opinion, *whatever works for you.*

Here's what I mean.

I'm sure you've looked at the multitude of real estate investment models out there. Student rentals, rent-to-owns, buy-fix-and-flips, buy-renovate-refi-and-holds, triplexes, fourplexes, apartments...the list goes on, and on.

And here's the deal.

There is ALWAYS someone crushing it in ANY ONE of these models.

You will ALWAYS meet someone who will tell you their "system" is the best.

Heck, if you ask me, buying and holding without doing ANYTHING is the best system.

That's because it works for my lazy investor lifestyle.

I'm NOT interested in getting my hands dirty, putting in a second suite to make more income, or anything like that.

I like to buy "ready to go" properties, put awesome tenants in who never leave, wait about five years, refi, take a nice chunk of change out and STILL have my properties. Then I lather, rinse, and repeat.

But that's ME.

And how I arrived at that is to look at my lifestyle TODAY, and NOT just the one I want tomorrow.

Because the reality is, our *tomorrow* lifestyle—the one where we have a yacht, a beach house, and flying to Paris for lunch—is a dream.

And there's nothing wrong with dreams...

But the truth is, a lot of real estate investors get HUNG UP on that future lifestyle... and the money it takes to LIVE that lifestyle, and never get started.

"Well, if I want to stop working and live on the beach, I need ten thousand dollars a month to do that...and that means I need a hundred properties by the end of this year... alright, so how do I do that?"

Or, "I want to make ten thousand dollars a month, so I need ten properties that will cash flow a thousand dollars every month. I've got no money, I don't know anyone with money, so how can I buy those properties this year with JV partners?"

What I'm telling you here is not unheard of.

People actually think this way.

And it's not their fault.

It may be the fault of the real estate investment seminar industry. It can be an industry that pumps people up, telling them they can do pretty much anything and everything.

Listen, I'm not here to deflate your dreams. Far from it.

I AM here to help you get them—but let's bring you back down to Earth for a moment and get you started.

Here's How:

Answer these following questions:

Step 1. What is my Current Lifestyle?

This is EXTREMELY important.

Because if you want to make fifty thousand dollars on a house you're going to renovate yourself and flip in six months, but you have a full-time job...HOW and WHEN are you going to do all this work?

At night when you come home from work and are exhausted? On the weekends that are the only time you have to unplug, recharge, and enjoy your life? Spend time with your friends, your family?

Are you truly equipped to do all the work it takes to renovate and flip a property in six months?

That's just ONE example.

So take into consideration what your life looks like RIGHT NOW, and how the real estate model you're looking at FITS—or doesn't.

Consider ALL the things you have to do in order to buy and maintain the real estate.

Step 2. What's Important Right Now?

To reach the lifestyle you want in the FUTURE, you need to figure out what the most important thing is NOW when it comes to real estate.

I challenge you to choose which of the following four are most important to you:

1. Cash Flow
2. Appreciation
3. Location
4. Tenant Profile

By answering Steps 1-2, you'll see how important it is to REALLY understand how these fit into your decisions because they relate back to Step 1.

Pre-Purchase Inspection Checklist for a FLIP

© Monika and Vaughan Jazyk

Inspection Date:

Property Address:

Property Description:

- ☐ Single
- ☐ Double/Duplex
- ☐ Triplex
- ☐ Multi-Unit
- ☐ Unfurnished
- ☐ Furnished

Other Property Particulars:

Examine Exterior of Home

1. Foundation

- ☐ Type of foundation:
- ☐ Condition (missing mortar in joints/open holes/cracks/other/damage)
  Comments:

2. Roof

- ☐ Type of roof:
- ☐ Shingles (missing pieces/cracking/damage)
- ☐ Framing (bowed sheathing/sagging ridge)
  Comments:

3. Windows

- ☐ Type of windows:
- ☐ Condition (caulking needed/broken glass/missing putty/missing latches)
  Comments:

4. Chimney

- ☐ Condition (missing mortar/damaged bricks/crumbling or cracking brickwork)
- ☐ Flashing (cemented over/open gaps or holes/needs overall repair)
  Comments:

5. Trim

☐ Condition (decaying wood/missing sections/peeling or chipped paint)

Comments:

6. Gutters

☐ Type of gutter:

☐ Condition (leaking/decaying/damaged/cracked)

Comments:

7. Siding

☐ Type of siding:

☐ Condition (decaying/cracked/dented/damaged)

☐ Repairs required (peeling paint/rusting/replace or repair missing sections)

Comments:

8. Downspouts

☐ Type:

☐ Condition (open seams/missing sections/rusting)

☐ Discharging to foundation (yes/no)

Comments:

9. Roof Vents

☐ Flashing (defective/needs repair/leaking)

☐ Condition (broken/damaged/missing)

Comments:

10. Entrances

- ☐ Condition of doors (fair/good/needs repair)
- ☐ Condition of steps (decaying/deteriorating brickwork/unsafe for use)
- ☐ Rails (yes/no)

    Comments:

11. Foundation Windows

- ☐ Type:
- ☐ Condition (decaying/rusting/broken)

    Comments:

12. Porches

- ☐ Location:
- ☐ Condition (decaying or damaged wood/trails of wood-boring insects/needs repair)

    Comments:

13. Skylights

- ☐ Damage (missing putty/cracked glass/decaying or damaged frame)

    Comments:

14. Garage

☐ Attached/Detached condition (needs repair/winterizing)

Comments:

15. Driveway

☐ Condition (cracking/decaying/heaving/needs repair-minor/major)

Comments:

16. Low Wood Members

☐ Location:

☐ Condition (decaying/insect activity/needs replacement)

Comments:

17. Grade

☐ Does surface water flow toward house/building?

☐ Location of dry walls (yes/no)

☐ Possibility of flooding (yes/no)

Comments:

18. Energy Losses

- ☐ Location(s):
- ☐ Type(s) (open gaps in siding/loose or missing trim/trim needs caulking/weather stripping needed around windows and doors)

  Comments:

19. Landscaping

- ☐ Overgrown shrubs (yes/no)
- ☐ Ivy on house (yes/no)
- ☐ Overhanging tree branches (yes/no)
- ☐ Location:

  Comments:

20. Fences

- ☐ Types:
- ☐ Condition (rusting/decaying)

  Comments:

21. Retaining Wall

- ☐ Type:
- ☐ Weep holes (yes/no)
- ☐ Condition (decaying/needs repair)

  Comments:

22. Paths

☐ Condition (settled/unsafe to use/cracked/damaged)

Comments:

23. Structural Pests

☐ Signs of pests (carpenter ants/termites/bed bugs/cockroaches/powder-post beetles)

☐ Location of damage or infestation:

Comments:

Mechanical Systems

1. Heating

- ☐ Type:
- ☐ Condition (functions/needs repairs)
- ☐ Type of fuel used (oil/gas)
- ☐ Firestopping needed (yes/no)
- ☐ Safety valves and shutoffs work properly (yes/no)
- ☐ Sufficient heat is produced (yes/no)
- ☐ Number of zones (1/2/3)
- ☐ Needs servicing or cleaning (yes/no)

  Comments:

2. Plumbing

- ☐ Drainage
- ☐ Water pressure (adequate/inadequate)
- ☐ Leaks (yes/no)
- ☐ Septic or cesspool system works properly (yes/no)
- ☐ Use of lead water lines or lead traps (yes/no)
- ☐ Sufficient amount of shutoff valves (yes/no)
- ☐ Shutoff valves working (yes/no)

  Comments:

3. Domestic Hot Water

- ☐ Type:
- ☐ Condition of tank (leaking/corrosion/needs replacement)
- ☐ Type of fuel (electricity/oil/gas)
- ☐ Safety valves working (yes/no)
- ☐ Size of tank:
- ☐ Sufficient hot water (yes/no)
- ☐ Location:

  Comments:

4. Electrical

- ☐ How many amps (60/100/150/200)
- ☐ Main disconnect working (yes/no)
- ☐ Serviced, grounded (yes/no)
- ☐ Use of (lamp cord/knob and tube wiring)
- ☐ Aluminum wiring (yes/no)
- ☐ Ground fault interrupters (yes/no)
- ☐ Plugs correctly wired (yes/no)

  Comments:

5. Solar

- ☐ Type (active/passive, heat/hot water)
- ☐ Working (yes/no)
- ☐ Fully insulated (yes/no)
- ☐ Condition of pipes:
- ☐ Solar collector location:

    Comments:

6. Air Conditioner

- ☐ Condition (good/fair/needs repair)
- ☐ Size of unit:
- ☐ Type (split/integral)
- ☐ Last servicing:

    Comments:

Basement Interior

1. Water Penetration

☐ Location:

☐ Efflorescence (yes/no)

☐ Sump pump working (yes/no)

Comments:

2. Cellar Floor

☐ Condition (holes/evidence of water, cracks/needs repair)

Comments:

3. Foundation Walls

☐ Accessible/Inaccessible

☐ Condition (poor/fair/good)

Comments:

4. Main Girder

☐ Condition (resting on foundation/needs repair)

☐ Evidence of deterioration, decay, or insect activity (yes/no)

☐ Extent:

Comments:

5. Insect Activity

- ☐ Type:
- ☐ Extent of damage:
- ☐ Location:

    Comments:

6. Floor Joists

- ☐ Condition (damaged, decaying, rotting, sagging)

    Comments:

7. Posts

- ☐ Type:
- ☐ Condition (fair/good/needs repairs)

    Comments:

8. Insulation

- ☐ Type:
- ☐ Condition:
- ☐ Location:
- ☐ Amount of insulation:
- ☐ Vapor barrier (yes/no)

    Comments:

9. Crawl Spaces (yes/no)

☐ Condition:

☐ Location:

Comments:

Attic

1. Insulation

- ☐ Type:
- ☐ Amount:
- ☐ Location:
- ☐ Condition (damaged, needs to be replaced)

    Comments:

2. Leaks

- ☐ Around the chimney (yes/no)
- ☐ Vent pipe leaks (yes/no)
- ☐ Daylight visible from attic (yes/no)
- ☐ Location:

    Comments:

3. Ventilation

- ☐ Kind (gable, roof, ridge, soffit)
- ☐ Needs repairs (yes/no)
- ☐ Sufficient ventilation (yes/no)
- ☐ Evidence of condensation (yes/no)

    Comments:

4. Improper Venting into Attic

☐ Location (bathroom vents, kitchen vents)

Comments:

5. Framing

☐ Condition (structurally sound/insect activity/decaying)

Comments:

Kitchen

1. Stove
- ☐ Type of fuel (electricity/gas/oil)
- ☐ Unit working (yes/no)
  Comments:

2. Sink
- ☐ Condition (poor/fair/good)
- ☐ Piping (damaged, leaks, needs replacement)
  Comments:

3. Ceilings
- ☐ Condition:
  Comments:

4. Appliances
- ☐ Types:
- ☐ Ages:
- ☐ Condition:
- ☐ Working (yes/no)
  Comments:

5. Walls

- ☐ Need repairs (yes/no)
- ☐ Location:

    Comments:

6. Floors

- ☐ Needs replacement (yes/no)

    Comments:

7. Ventilation and Light

- ☐ Adequate
- ☐ Inadequate

    Comments:

8. Heat (yes/no)

Comments:

9. Cabinets and Counter Space

- ☐ Adequate
- ☐ Inadequate

    Comments:

10. Electrical Outlets

☐ Sufficient

☐ Needs more outlets

   Comments:

Bathrooms

1. Fixtures

☐ Condition (poor/fair/good)

☐ Leaks (yes/no)

☐ Damaged or chipped fixtures (yes/no)

☐ Location:

☐ Faucets dripping (yes/no)

Comments:

2. Ventilation

☐ Type (mechanical vents/windows)

Comments:

3. Ceilings

☐ In need of repairs (yes/no)

Comments:

4. Ground Fault Interrupter

☐ Existing (yes/no)

☐ Working (yes/no)

Comments:

5. Water Pressure

- ☐ Adequate
- ☐ Needs repair

    Comments:

6. Tile

- ☐ Condition (missing/chipped/broken/falling off of walls)

    Comments:

7. Heat (yes/no)

    Comments:

8. Floors

- ☐ Condition (tile pulling up/needs replacement/deteriorating or decaying)

    Comments:

9. Walls

- ☐ Condition (damaged walls from water/needs repair/loose plaster)
- ☐ Location for repairs:

    Comments:

10. Drainage

☐ Normal

☐ Sluggish

Comments:

Rooms

1. Walls

- ☐ Condition (needs repair/missing sections/holes)
- ☐ Location for repairs:

  Comments:

2. Windows

- ☐ New storm windows needed?
- ☐ Condition (need repairs/general tightening up)

  Comments:

3. Heating

- ☐ Register/Radiator/None

  Comments:

4. Closets

- ☐ Sufficient size/Insufficient size
- ☐ Needs more closets or closet space

  Comments:

5. Ceilings

☐ Condition (sagging plaster/water stains/cracks/damaged areas)

Comments:

6. Floors

☐ Condition (refinish/install new floor/replace carpeting)

Comments:

7. Doors

☐ Condition (damaged/needs repair/missing)

Comments:

8. Electrical

☐ Overhead lights

☐ Needs additional outlets

Comments:

Other: Fireplace and/or Stove

1. Safety Hazards

☐ Location:

☐ Types:

Comments:

2. Condition of Flue Pipe

☐ Poor/Fair/Good/Needs replacement

Comments:

3. Needs Cleaning

☐ Yes/No

☐ Last cleaning/servicing:

Comments:

4. Permit for Stove

☐ Yes/No

Comments:

5. Proximity to Combustible Materials

☐ Location:

Comments:

Construction Budget Download

Monika and Vaughan Jazyk

Real Estate Investment Specialists and Wealth Builders

Monika and Vaughan Jazyk chose real estate as an investment vehicle to build income and long-term wealth for their growing family. After a tumultuous two years of actively investing in a wide range of real estate investment strategies, Monika and Vaughan identified specific real estate models they used to create a successful portfolio and a lifestyle of freedom for themselves and their four young children.

Monika and Vaughan are the founders and owners of RPI Education, a real estate investment corporation that helps real people build REAL life through real estate. With a variety of resources and programs, including digital courses, live events, memberships, and personal coaching programs, their full-service team of financial experts, wealth builders and real estate investment specialists are dedicated toward educating and empowering everyday people to learn how to invest like the top 2%. To date, RPI Education has assisted thousands of investors in finding turn-key investment properties, growing their funds in alternative investments, and providing them with real estate education.

Monika and Vaughan are passionate about helping other people create wealth through real estate and alternative investments so they can reach their personal and financial goals. They spend their days seeking joy in everyday life through travel, philanthropy, friends, and most importantly, family.

For more information on RPI Education events and consulting services, visit www.rpieducation.com.

RPI Education

RPinvestments.ca
info@RPIinvestments.ca
1 888-519-3224

We are a full-service team of financial experts, wealth builders, and real estate investment specialists dedicated toward educating and empowering everyday people to learn how to invest like the top 2%.

We help you with every aspect of real estate investing, acting as your one stop shop!

At RPI Education, we offer a variety of resources and programs to empower you so you can start building wealth in your life TODAY. We believe that real estate is the #1 asset class and help our members learn to build wealth through real estate and alternative investment products.

Working with us is easy! We offer digital courses, live events, memberships, and personal coaching programs to help you start investing differently and create your life of freedom. Our team members include wealth advisors, real estate agents, mortgage brokers, home inspectors, contractors, property managers, insurance agents (Property and Life), lawyers, and accountants.

We are the world's fastest growing real estate investment community. RPI Education has helped thousands of people across the globe achieve freedom in their lives and continues to empower REAL people to put finances at the forefront and learn to invest differently. We have online courses available on our website, as well as different levels of membership and coaching services offering ongoing support. We host regular events at each of our chapters across Canada, US, Europe, and Australia.